KILLERS AT LARGE

Unsolved Mysteries through the Ages, around the Humber

by

A. A. CLARKE

ARTON BOOKS 1996

Published by Arton Books
3, Dominican Walk, Beverley, HU17 0HF

Copyright © 1996 by A. A. Clarke

*Printed by Clifford Ward & Co.
(Bridlington) Ltd.,
55 West Street, Bridlington, East Yorkshire,
YO15 3DZ*

ISBN 0 9522163 6 1

ACKNOWLEDGEMENT

I wish to acknowledge the help and assistance I have received in producing this book from many people. In particular my thanks go to the staffs of the *Grimsby Evening Telegraph* and *Scunthorpe Evening Telegraph* for their welcome and the facilities and encouragement they gave me. My thanks are also due to the staffs of the Local Studies Library at Hull, the County Archives in Beverley and Beverley and Hull Reference Libraries. A special thank you goes to Tony Leonard, Chief Constable of Humberside and my friends in the Police Service who gave me invaluable research facilities. Lastly but by no means least I would like to thank those relatives and friends of persons the subject of these mysteries, who felt able to help me.

Photographs from the *Hull Daily Mail*, *Grimsby Evening Telegraph* and *Scunthorpe Evening Telegraph* are reproduced with permission from the Editors of those papers.

CONTENTS

page

Author's Note 6
Preface 7

Elizabeth Parker, Hull 11
William Rothwell, Hull 14
Mary Langley, Preston 16
Anne Todd, Cottingham 26

David Ombler, Hull 30
Samuel Smith, Hull 36
Oswald Walker, Hull 43

Frederick Wilkinson, Hull 56
Frederick Dean, Hull 60
Gloria Bielby, Bilton 62
Christine Markham, Scunthorpe 70
Evelyn Rounding, Hull 75

Evelyn Edwards, Hull 80
Robert Stephenson, Barton 85
Walter Taylor, Scunthorpe 93
Olive Wilkinson, Grimsby 98
Susan Drury, Scunthorpe 102
Florence Mills, Scunthorpe 107
Keith Slater, Hessle 112

Conclusions 118

AUTHOR'S NOTE

The events in this book have been separated into four distinct sections. The first deals with murders in Victorian and Edwardian times when fewer details were recorded if the mystery remained undetected.

The second section deals with the cases of three Hull businessmen who were killed in brutal fashion between 1914 and 1936 and whose murderer was never found.

Thirdly are the sinister disappearances of people of all ages who vanished never to be seen or heard of again.

Finally the largest section is devoted to murders in modern times and which, despite every effort by highly trained police, have never been solved.

Certain cases in which the investigation is still 'live' have been omitted at the request of police.

PREFACE

In a small dusty corner of the headquarters building of Humberside Police in Hull are the files of undetected murders and other mysteries both old and new. Protected by heavy wire mesh and padlocked against the curious, the faded names of men and women, who have mysteriously vanished or been brutally done to death, can be seen on the shelves. In the farthest, darkest corner one can just see a section marked faintly with the words 'Murders pre-1917'. Still they are kept, hoping some miracle might reveal the truth. The papers within are crackly and yellowing with age but the clear copper plate handwriting provides a measure of the great care taken with their records by previous generations of police investigators.

People have always viewed homicide, the unlawful killing of one human being by another, as the most repugnant of crimes and have expected the forces of law and order to move heaven and earth to bring killers to justice.

But an examination of the reports makes one wonder how many murderers escaped from the law and how many of the sudden deaths which received scant attention, were in fact murders!!

Even today, with modern, highly trained police forces, sophisticated equipment, forensic science and breathtaking communications, while murders will almost certainly be recognised and treated as such, many of the worst can still remain worryingly undetected. Killers escape!!

As late as the 1960s most police forces in England and Wales had little or no expertise in investigating such serious matters and C1 department, other wise known as the murder squad at New Scotland Yard was constantly in demand to help their provincial colleagues. Home Office encouraged their use by funding the costs of the London detectives provided their assistance was requested within 48 hours of the crime being discovered. This stipulation was to prevent proud and independent forces from attempting to solve the crime themselves, only to call for the 'Yard' in desperation when their own efforts had been unsuccessful and often when the trail had gone cold!

Prior to Queen Victoria coming to the throne, there was no Scotland Yard and, apart from the few Bow Street Runners, little in the way of a police force. In those early days, the Authority responsible for investigating sudden deaths on behalf of the Crown was, and still is today, the Coroner.

The origins of this particular office are in the 12th Century when the Crown needed money urgently as the Crusades were becoming an intolerable burden on the Royal Exchequer.

Sheriffs in counties were very powerful and carried out many Judicial duties including the collection of fines. Many of them were also extremely devious characters (witness the Sheriff of Nottingham in the saga of Robin Hood!!). Much of the money collected never reached the coffers of the Crown and crimes which should have been reported to the Monarch were concealed if it suited the Sheriffs' purpose.

To overcome the machinations of these dubious officials, in 1149 three knights and a clerk were appointed to be Coronators or Coroners in each county "to keep the pleas of the Crown". Over the years their main duty has resolved into being the enquiring into violent and unnatural deaths.

One can only guess at the situation which existed before the arrival of newspapers, suffice to say that looking back at some of the verdicts of Coroners' Courts as recently as Edwardian and Victorian days, gives rise to a feeling of disquiet. An alarming number of sudden deaths were simply written off as 'cause unknown!!'

Many dead bodies were recovered from the rivers and docks in Hull. One was reported as having severe head injuries but again the verdict was 'cause of injury unknown' *Hopefully not a matter which would have escaped so easily today!!* How many of the bodies had been pushed in or held under??? How many were killed before being put into the water???

Many were the strange verdicts by Juries at Coroners' Courts in the 19th century, for example:

> "he died from exhaustion caused by a large carbuncle"
>
> "she died from an overdose of Godfrey's cordial."
>
> "he died from inflammation of the bowel caused by another boy throwing him down in the street!"

When proper, full time forces were established around the middle of the nineteenth century few were equipped either by training or experience to deal with serious homicides.

Forces were reluctant to reveal their shortcomings and in 1922 Home Office asked Hull Police why their Homicide return for 1912 failed to record the death of a Russian seaman at Victoria Dock in the city.

The dead man, a fireman on the Russian ship S.S. *Arcturus* was in dock in Hull and the crew started to hold an impromptu dance on the dock side. A fight developed between the deceased and a sailor from another ship during which blows were struck with a pit prop. The name of the attacker was known but he was never brought to justice. The Coroner's jury returned a verdict of wilful murder but still nothing was done and it appears police were happy to try and sweep the matter under the carpet! Considerable embarrassment would have been caused when Home Office found out ten years later!!

Until well after the conclusion of the Second World War and in some areas not until the arrival of the 1970s, many forces had little or no expertise in such matters and the services of Scotland Yard were always in demand in the provinces.

Today's problem in tackling a difficult murder case is no longer a lack of skill or technical expertise, it is the lack of money. Policemen have become incredibly expensive and the overtime necessary to investigate a serious murder case, makes it hard for those in charge to afford the necessary resources.

Whatever the problems however, detectives in British police forces have always considered it a matter of very considerable pride to clear up a murder case and many are prepared to work for no extra pay just to achieve the satisfaction of a detection. Sadly, despite such dedication, despite all the modern scientific assistance, some serious cases still go undetected. It is to recall some of the more interesting ones that this book has been written.

LOCAL MURDERS
IN VICTORIAN/EDWARDIAN TIMES

Many local folk died in suspicious circumstances before the First
World War and the mysteries of some of these deaths have never
been solved.

RENNARD BEFORE THE MAGISTRATES.

RELEASE OF THE ACCUSED.

THE SCENE IN COURT.

ARREST OF A HULL MAN ON SUSPICION.

VIOLENT ATTACK UPON YOUNG LADIES.

THREATENED WITH A CLASP KNIFE.

THE HOME WHICH THE POOR GIRL NEVER REACHED

[Photographed and Engraved by our own Artists.]

THE SCENE OF THE MURDER

SUSPICIOUS DEATH.

ELIZABETH PARKER

The many poorer people in Hull lived in "Courts" which were clusters of the very poorest housing, often consisting of one small room for a family. Conditions were filthy, damp, and often rooms were below ground level and subject to regular flooding. There were Courts within courts and further Courts within those — the whole constructions teemed with all forms of human life.

Dock Labourer William Parker lived in the teeming North Court, off Dock Street, in the City in 1854. Living with him were his wife, a male lodger and the Parker's pretty 14-year old daughter Elizabeth. The young girl, as well as being pretty, was also a lively and completely street-wise kid. While her clothes may have been tattered, her youth and bright personality made her an attractive young girl.

Mrs. Maudsley kept a shop in Dock Street and, most of her customers had difficulty in paying for their goods. One of her best customers was Mrs. Steele and this lady was so highly regarded that Mrs. Maudsley had no compunction in allowing her credit for groceries. Young Elizabeth Parker often ran errands to the shop for Mrs. Steele.

One Wednesday afternoon Elizabeth called at the shop and asked for some bacon and cooked brawn for Mrs. Steele. This was duly supplied and the girl left the shop. Later in the afternoon Mrs. Steele called to settle her account but to Mrs. Maudsley's surprise, denied asking for the brawn and refused to pay for it.

The doughty shop keeper lost no time in finding Mrs. Parker and informing her of the situation. As soon as Elizabeth arrived home her mother took her back to the shop to get the matter sorted out, having first informed Mrs. Steele where she was going.

Questioned by the three women Elizabeth sniffed tearfully but wouldn't say anything. Eventually she burst into tears and while the three women were talking, left the shop unnoticed and returned to her home.

Mr. Parker was told of the situation when he arrived home that evening. He was very cross and insisted his wife take Elizabeth back to Mrs. Maudsley's and settle the matter once and for all. The women set off but a few minutes later his wife returned and said that the girl had run away from her on the way to the shop.

Time passed and when Elizabeth did not return her parents and the lodger went to look for her. Finding no sign of the girl at her usual haunts and becoming very concerned about their only daughter, the Parkers went to see the police who circulated Elizabeth's description to all their patrols.

At about 10 o'clock the following morning, 12-year old Lucy Forsey, one of Elizabeth's friends, was with a group of girls when she saw Elizabeth in Lowgate. Not knowing she had been reported missing, Lucy was surprised when Elizabeth said she was emigrating to America in the ship *Pioneer* which was in dock at the time. Later Mr. Parker came along asking about his daughter and Lucy told him of her meeting with Elizabeth. Her story was corroborated by one of the other girls in the group — Sarah Wrigglesworth.

Mr. Parker immediately relayed this information to the police and Constable Hepworth was despatched to check the *Pioneer*. After questioning, the steward on the vessel admitted a girl answering Elizabeth's description had slept on the deck the previous night. The Constable searched the vessel, found nothing and, as it was due to leave, the vessel was allowed to sail.

Later the same day 15-year old Thomas Hall was messing about on the bank of the river when he saw what he thought was a bundle of rags. Poking it with his stick he soon realised he had found a body! Horrified, he ran to raise the alarm.

Still dressed in the clothes she had been wearing when last seen, the body of Elizabeth Parker was carried gently to her home by four policemen.

Doctor King, a local physician was called by police to examine the body and he concluded the girl had certainly not been in the water for anything like the length of time she had been missing. In his opinion she had not been sexually assaulted although he thought she could have had voluntary sex. She had died of suffocation although he could find no trace of strangulation. The strangest of his conclusions was that the girl's body had a lot of injuries consistent with either being badly scratched with finger nails or being rolled in gravel, or both. Highly suspicious!

A mere fourteen days after she was last seen alive, the Inquest on Elizabeth Parker was held and a verdict recorded as "found dead with marks of violence". There is no record of any major police enquiry into the matter!!

Even the most amateurish sleuth would have given some more attention to the ship *Pioneer* and its crew. The dead girl tells her friend she is going to America on it and the steward admits she slept on deck. She must therefore have had some contact with one or more of the crew. Presumably the "gravel" idea came to the doctor because specks of it were sticking into the skin. If so was there any gravel near to the ship?

There can be very little doubt this young girl was murdered and the murderer was unlikely to have been very far away from the ship *Pioneer*! A sad story!

WILLIAM ROTHWELL

Fifty-seven years old William Rothwell was a well known figure in Hull. A friendly and harmless itinerant who made a meagre living from begging and from making and selling artificial wooden flowers, most of the money he made was quickly disposed of in one of the many city centre hostelries he frequented. On 26th July 1867 he was in the Hamburgh Castle public house, sitting in a corner and half asleep.

A noisy group of young fishermen, recently home and with money to spend, were drinking in the Inn and turned their attention to the half stupefied beggar. First they took his pathetic bundle of wooden flowers and, breaking the stems, stuck them into his clothing from his cap down to his boots.

Grinning foolishly the old man made no attempt to stop them.

"Give us a song Billy", they howled. "Come on, stand up and give us a dance!" The group staggered round, pulling at the tattered

figure trying to get him to his feet. Failing to get him to stand they released him and he dropped to the floor in a heap muttering incoherently. Nobody interfered. Fishermen were known to be trouble when they were just back from sea!!

A short respite while they recharged their glasses and the men returned to the recumbent figure. A few desultory shouts and kicks failed to waken the man and interest was beginning to wane when someone suggested they "light him up!"

"Yes, yes" came the growling cry and one of the group staggered to the bar and shouted "Give us a bottle of whisky" jangling a handful of sovereigns. The bottle handed over, the man took a swig and handed it to his mates who did likewise. They approached the beggar and one poured some of the spirit over him. "Bring the bloody candle", he laughed and putting the flame to Rothwell's jacket he roared as the blue flame quickly spread along the body.

The men howled with glee as the flames quickly spread through the tinder dry clothes but the noise was hushed when with a piercing shriek the body tried to rise from the floor. Slumping back down the figure writhed in the flames and one of the now silent men gave a hollow laugh, a mixture of bravado and fear.

As the flames engulfed the twitching, howling figure, the by now frightened landlord rushed round with a bucket of water and, shouldering the fishermen aside, threw it onto the burning man.

A doctor was summoned and the fishermen began quickly leaving. By the time the medical man arrived the charred figure had become motionless. William Rothwell was pronounced dead and a constable was summoned. The rest of the customers quietly left the Inn.

Questioned by the constable the landlord professed ignorance of the affair saying the first he knew something was wrong was when someone had shouted that Billy Rothwell was on fire. He said he had put the flames out with a bucket of water but that it had been too late to save the old man.

The constable showed little interest when he knew the identity of the dead man, he merely noted details for the Coroner and made arrangements for the body to be removed. A police cart was brought to the scene and the remains of Bill Rothwell were removed. As he was taken away a little trail of blackened wooden flowers fell slowly onto the cobbles. It was the only floral tribute he was likely to get!!

An Inquest was held and on the advice of the Coroner based on the best evidence available to him, the verdict was that William Rothwell died by accidentally setting himself on fire!

MARY JANE LANGLEY

The Langleys were a quiet, ordinary family of conscientious farmers working the flat Holderness land at West Field Farm, Marsh Lane, Preston. The lane was known locally as Long Lane. Mr. and Mrs. Langley had two grown up children, 21-year old William, their son and heir and their beloved 19-year old Mary Jane.

The year was 1891, Great Britain was at the height of her power, the Boers might still be resisting in South Africa; there might be industrial unrest in Hull docks; but little of this affected the peaceful seasonal routine on the Langley farm.

It was summer, the end of July and time for the Langleys to pay their rent. On Thursday morning Mr. and Mrs. Langley set off for Driffield to see their landlord and do some shopping and told William and Mary to look after the farm until they returned.

Not long after their departure Mary told William she wanted to go into Hull to get her photo taken by Mr. Edmunds at his studio in

West Field Farm and Long Lane.

16

Witham. She left the farm at 12 noon and promised to catch the train back which would arrive at the local Marfleet station at 2.30 pm.

She had no fear of walking along Long Lane although she knew of its reputation as a lonely place frequented by men from the Southcoates area of Hull who were known to visit there for "peculiar reasons of their own!!" as the Press were later to describe it!

The afternoon passed peacefully and rather lazily in the warm sunshine and when Mr. and Mrs. Langley got back at 6 o'clock they were annoyed but not concerned to find Mary missing. William told them where she had gone and she had promised to be back definitely by 4 o'clock to take the wages to the workmen in the fields. The family presumed she had stayed in Hull where she was known to be courting a boy named Arthur Hall. She may even have gone by train with him to Cleethorpes to visit a girl who had been Mrs. Langley's charwoman for two years. Mr. Langley had recently found a letter to Mary from her boyfriend offering to take her on such a trip. On the other hand she might have stopped off to see friends in Preston or Hedon. She was nineteen years of age after all!!

The next day dawned and when there was still no sign of Mary the family began to worry. Both Mr. Langley and William went to Hull and while the father visited Mary's friends, William checked with the Witham photograher. When they returned to the farm the father had nothing to report but William could confirm that Mary had been photographed as she intended.

Mr. Langley decided to return to Hull, collect the photograph, and inform the police. Before he left he nervously told his wife of a bizarre dream he had experienced a night or so previously. He related how he dreamt a large black dog leapt out from a hole under the bridge over a drainage ditch about threee-quarters of a mile from their farm in Marsh Lane.

He would pass the bridge on his way to the railway station and out of curiosity would have a good look there. With a sense of foreboding, he approached the bridge and looked into the ditch which was dry as usual in the summer. To his horror he was immediately confronted with the sight of his daughter's body. It was partly hidden under a hedge at the top of the ditch and her head was resting on her umbrella. The distraught man could see that his daughter's throat had been savagely cut and her clothes had been turned up to her knees. Her jacket and hat were some distance away as was a wet handkerchief. Footprints were visible by the body and

Mary Jane Langley.

it appeared a dog had also been in the ditch. He knew she was dead but nevertheless rushed back to the farm to send for help.

Doctor Souter from Hedon arrived and confirmed life extinct and felt there was no chance the wound could have been self-inflicted.

The local police were informed and eventually between 4 pm and 5 pm the body was taken to the Langley's farm. A gold watch and albert and a purse were missing.

Superintendent John Burniston arrived from Sproatley in his horse and trap and together with Sergeant John Sales from Hedon, took charge of the case but were soon to be scathingly criticised by the Press. The *Hull Times* wrote:

> "The East Riding Constabulary showed a glaring incapacity to cope with the murder. Superintendent Burniston of Sproatley evidently did not realise the tragedy called for prompt and immediate action, because it was fully 9 pm before he bothered to inform Hull police. The first information the Borough had was via the *Hull Times*, a special edition of which was brought out at 8 pm giving details of the terrible affair."

However, enquiries were started both in Hull and the county areas with the Borough force assisting their County colleagues. Major Bower, Chief Constable of the East Riding force visited the scene and asked to be kept in touch with the case. An ex military man with little or no previous police experience he was still smarting from Home Office criticism of the way the rape of a young girl at Rillington had been handled some ten years earlier. He nearly lost his job then!!

The place where the body had been discovered soon became a popular visiting spot with hundreds of ghoulish persons travelling, particularly from Hull, to stare at the ditch where the young woman's body had been found.

Mary's boyfriend, William Hall was seen and could account for his whereabouts and also said he had not seen Mary for some days. Mr. Edmunds the photographer confirmed the girl had been photographed, had paid 1/6d and left his studio about 3 pm. More significantly William Leckonby, gatekeeper at Marfleet station, recalled a girl arriving on the 5.10 pm train and setting off across the fields towards Marsh or Long Lane.

The groom to Mr. Sam Lear mentioned seeing a suspicious man with an Airedale dog in the lane on the afternoon in question and the *Hull Times* newspaper claimed a Mrs. Clark, landlady of the Nag's Head pub in Preston was so frightened by a man who called, that being on her own as her husband had gone to Aldbrough Flower Show, she asked a neighbour to stay with her. The man left at a time which would have coincided with the arrival of the 5.10 pm train!

Working on the description of the man with the Airedale, police suspicions fell on John Rennard well known in local boxing circles as middleweight champion Jack Renny!! He was very popular and very successful but believed to act strangely when in drink.

Sergeant Sales and Detective Sergeant Rutherford of Hull established Rennard was drinking in the Nag's Head in Holderness Road with his mates and sent a message asking him to step outside. Witnesses were later to say that this message made him look very worried indeed.

He was taken to the main Hull police station in Parliament Street and was interrogated about his movements on the day in question. He said he had left his home at 4 Mawer's Terrace, Courtney Street,Hull at about 10.30 am

John Rennard.

19

in the morning with his red coloured rough-haired terrier, walked across fields, until he eventually arrived at the Nag's Head, Preston at about 4.30 pm. He had a couple of pints and left the Inn at about 5.20. He then walked down Long Lane, across the bridge over the ditch where the body had been found and made his way to the Nags Head on Holderness Road by about 6.40 pm.

He was taken to his home and asked to produce the clothes he had been wearing on the day in question. He handed over a pair of moleskins which Sergeant Sales thought had blood stains on! Police were beginning to feel they were definitely making progress!! They calculated that even if his timings were correct he could still have reached the bridge where the murder took place, before or at the same time as Mary if she had arrived at Marfleet at 5.10 pm.

The fact that Mrs. Esther Nicholson, of the Blacksmith's Arms in Preston came forward and said she thought she saw Mary arrive at Marfleet on the 2 o'clock train from Southcoates and saw her walk off across the fields towards Long Lane followed by two men and one woman perplexed the investigators but failed to shake their faith in Rennard as the main suspect.

Tuesday saw a special sitting of the Sproatley Magistrates at the offices of G. R. Park & Sons in Bishop Lane, Hull. Present were the chief constables of both Hull and the East Riding.

John Rennard was brought into the Court with another man named Jim Parkin. Parkin, a married man working as an oil miller and living in Aldbrough Street in the east of Hull was alleged to have attacked a Miss Folkard and a Miss Ransome, both from Sutton, as they were walking to Church and only three days after the murder. He had thrown one woman into a ditch and threatened her with a knife. He had only stopped the attack when she told him where her purse was. Police said their enquiries had eliminated him from the murder enquiry. Some observers at the time wondered whether this was simply because they had their minds fixed on Rennard.

Local interest in the case was intense and the court was crowded. At no time did Rennard show the slightest emotion and one press reporter could not resist noting his strange eyes, "constantly rolling upwards and with a completely empty look in them".

Superintendent Burniston presented the case for the police and Mr. Hare, a Solicitor appeared to represent Rennard. The reports reveal an embarrassingly incompetent performance by the worthy Superintendent as the following passage shows.

The proceedings started with Sergeant Sales of Hedon giving evidence about Rennard's arrest and then reading Rennard's statement about his movements....

Supt. Burniston, interrupting when the Sergeant got to Rennard's alleged movements near Long Lane.

"By going that way would he have had to pass the place where the murder was committed?"

Serg. Sales: "If he left Preston at twenty-past-five he would have got to the scene by a quarter-to-six!"

Magistrate. "You say *where the murder was committed* Superintendent! Do you know where it was?"

Supt. Burniston: "Well, where we suppose it was!"

A few moments later Mr. Hare asked casually why his client was in Court. "To answer the charge of murder!" puffed the Superintendent. "But he hasn't been *charged* with anything, has he?" the solicitor asked politely. "Ah yes, well", mumbled the Superintendent, "he's been arrested on suspicion. We'd best get him charged here and now!"

Sergeant Sales gave further evidence about the finding of the body, about Rennard's arrest, and about the trousers from Rennard's house which had blood stains on. In answer to cross examination he agreed the stains were mostly on the inside of the trousers and when asked if the blood had been analysed he admitted it had not.

The Court agreed to remand Rennard in custody for a week when a further hearing would be held to decide whether there was sufficient evidence to send the matter for trial.

Rennard's wife was later tackled by reporters about the blood on the trousers and subsequently printed her claim that her husband refused to wear underpants and that he suffered from heat spots on his legs which he constantly scratched and blood spots were always on his clothes!

The great crowd in and around the Court all appeared to support Rennard, although those inside were restrained by their awe of the atmosphere of the Court. Discussion was rife and with the normal perverse nature of human beings, although they mostly liked Rennard, the thought that he might be a murderer tickled their imaginations.

The Press, whose activities in the case seem to have been more energetic than those of the police, were intrigued by having such a dramatic case in their area. Not only did their reporters work with great diligence, the paper also encouraged people with information to come to them. So they were able to cause a great stir by printing a report that a Mr. Burn, tram conductor in Hull told them he picked a passenger up at Newlands on Thursday evening, the day of the murder. Mr. Burn claimed that as the tram was about to leave Newlands at 6.20 pm he was hailed by a man running from the direction of Sutton. The man had a dog and appeared very much out of breath. When the conductor asked for his fare he noticed the man had a badly cut hand which he was trying to bind up. He also noticed his waistcoat was covered with blood.

The information was passed to police but although they showed interest it does not appear the man was ever traced.

A hastily prepared file of papers was sent by the Chief Constable to the Director of Public Prosecutions in London and he in turn instructed Mr. Wray, a local Hull Solicitor to undertake the case on his behalf.

Superintendent Burniston and Sergeant Sales meanwhile visited Rennard in Hull prison and officially took possession of his boots. With a warder accompanying them the two officers returned to the ditch at Long Lane where the body had been found and tried to match Rennard's boots with footmarks at the scene.

That the attempt to obtain such evidence was rather late would be obvious to the most casual observer but the means by which they tried to match the boots were so pathetically elementary it defied belief and became a matter of considerable comment at the subsequent Court hearing! They were unable to make a cast of any footprint near to the body because these had all been obliterated by people tramping over the ground. Finding one nearby which they had no reason to believe was the murderer's they nevertheless tried to fit the boot into it. When this failed they measured the mark by breaking twigs to the same length and breadth and felt these measurements corresponded to the prisoner's boot!!

Meanwhile more evidence was forthcoming to support Mrs. Nicholson's story that Mary had been on the 2 o'clock train, rather than the later one. Only one ticket had been sold that afternoon from Southcoates to Marfleet and none had been sold for the 5 o'clock train.

The Church Institute, Preston was the scene of the adjourned

Coroner's Inquest into Mary Jane's death, with the District Coroner for Holderness, Henry Birks, taking the evidence. For three days the Jury heard the facts of the case and ultimately decided that Mary Jane Langley had been murdered by some person or persons unknown.

The day after the Inquest finished the Magistrate re-assembled for a Special Court at Sessions House Hull, to consider committing John Rennard for trial for murder! Mr. Maxted presided, Mr. Wray appeared for H.M. Treasury and Mr. Hare was defence solicitor. The Court was again packed to overflowing with many unable to get in and with ladies of some standing engaging in the most unladylike jostling for seats in the Womens' Gallery!

Many of the men present were Rennard's associates who, reports said, "assembled in strong force to smile encouragingly upon the man in the dock and to clap him on the shoulder should he become a free man again!"

At the outset, most of the onlookers had already made up their minds that the Prosecution case was not worth a candle and consequently no evidence would be offered and that Rennard would be discharged.

It was a hot day and the atmosphere in the courtroom was overpowering. Women fanned themselves and men wiped foreheads and faces with coloured handkerchiefs. The clock struck eleven and suddenly all went still as footsteps were heard from beneath the dock. Suddenly Rennard's head appeared and a sigh rose from the galleries. Impassive as always, Rennard walked into the dock apparently oblivious of those present.

The Magistrates entered and the hearing began. Immediately there was a sensation! Mr. Wray rose to his feet but instead of requesting the case be withdrawn, he said he would be asking for a further remand in custody in view of sensational new evidence!! The crowd gasped! Was the boxer guilty after all? The police wouldn't be asking for further remands unless they had some pretty impressive new evidence. What could it be?

The Prosecutor continued by saying that he would be calling important evidence about the blood on the trousers and about footprints at the scene.

He called Sergeant Sales to give evidence about the finding of the corpse, the arrest of Rennard, and the finding of the trousers, but Mr. Wray got into considerable difficulties when dealing with the footprint. The Sergeant admitted he had not dealt with it until four days after the body had been found. He agreed with the defence that a considerable number of people head been tramping in the area in the meantime. Yes, the footprint he found *was* some way from where the body had been discovered but having Rennard's boot in his possession he thought perhaps he should first make an impression with that, near to where the suspect footprint was, to visually compare them!!! Deciding that they looked similar he then measured the suspect footprint with a twig he broke from the hedge!!! He agreed that the boots they had recovered from Rennard were of a very common make!! The crowd were agog at this evidence which they could see was terribly flawed.

Apparently oblivious to the increasing restlessness of the Magistrates the worthy Prosecutor pressed on and called Mr. Bayles an Analyst who had examined the trousers. This turned out a further disaster for the hapless Prosecution.

Far from being a sensational witness for the Crown, the Analyst turned out to be a gift for the Defence. He was unable to say if the blood was human or animal, he agreed with the defence that it could well have come from eczema and, to cap it all he felt anyone who had murdered someone in the circumstances of the present case could not have avoided having very considerable blood on his clothes. Not just a few spots!!

The pathetic Prosecution went on for a little longer when the patience of the Magistrate finally gave out and Mr. Maxted suggested that if the Prosecuting Solicitor had nothing more substantial to connect Rennard than the fact that he had been in the area, possibly about the time of the murder, then the case should be dismissed.

Mr. Wray responded by saying he had some vital evidence still to produce and, when this turned out to be merely a number of people who claimed to have seen the dead girl arrive at Marfleet Railway Station, at contradictory times, the Crown at last seemed to realise that it was all over.

Defending Solicitor then made an eloquent and masterly speech. He first demolished the footprint and bloodstain evidence and concluded by saying the only evidence against his client was that he had been in the area at about 5 or 6 in the late afternoon on the day in question. Mrs. Clarke from the Nags Head at Preston was called and denied Press stories that she had been frightened of Rennard when he called in the Inn. "And how?" demanded the Advocate, "could young Mary Jane have been about at 5 pm or after when no tickets had been sold from Southcoates to Marfleet for the 5 o'clock train but significantly one had been sold for the 2 o'clock!! The murdered girl should have been home well before Rennard had reached the district!" He paused and said, "I suggest Your Worships there is no case on which to commit my client for trial!" He sat down and Mr. Maxted after a brief consultation with his two fellow Magistrates announced the Court found there was insufficient evidence to commit the Prisoner.

Rennard was released amid scenes of wild rejoicing. Outside the Court a cab was commandeered and the horse removed from the shafts by his friends who proceeded to pull him all the way to his home.

An Inquest into Mary Jane's murder was resumed a few days later and on the Coroner's advice the Jury decided not to commit Rennard themselves but to return an 'open' verdict.

Next day police announced a £20 reward for information leading to the recovery of the property stolen from Mary Jane's body.

So ended a sad case for the East Riding Constabulary, a vicious murder in rural Holderness but close to the burgeoning Borough of Hull. The officers who dealt with the matter would have tried their hardest to solve a case which would have been quite outside their experience. Not only were they untrained for such investigations, the technical back-up was rudimentary and unless they could literally 'beat' a confession from a suspect they were lost!

The days of calling in Scotland Yard for provincial murders as a matter of course had not arrived otherwise a different result may have emerged.

Did Rennard commit the murder? Was the dishevelled man on the tram connected? No-one was ever brought to justice for one of the most celebrated but unresolved murder cases in the history of Holderness! Somewhere a murderer lived after cutting short a blameless young life!!

ANNE TODD

Anne Todd, a seventy-eight years old widow of a farmer died on 1st February 1901 in the house of her brother-in-law in Anlaby Road, Hull. The date, as well as the cause of death, assumed great significance as we shall see later.

On the morning of Sunday 25th February the previous year, she had been living in Cottingham. Although elderly she was fiercely independent and while she employed a part-time servant, insisted on doing much of the housework herself.

Her neighbours were aware of her practice of rising early in the mornings it was therefore a surprise for Henry Ross, a school attendance officer who lived opposite her in Hallgate, to notice that the curtains were still down and that there was no smoke rising from the chimney. Most odd he thought!! but quite happy to mind his own business. It was not until his wife had almost badgered him to death that he agreed to go and see if their elderly neighbour was alright.

He found that the front door of her house was locked but on going round the back he found the door open and, lying in a heap in the corner of the kitchen was the body of Mrs. Todd. Mr. Ross noted with horror that her face was badly swollen and cut. The room was in a terrible mess and there was a large pool of blood on the floor with a set of dentures resting in it.

Assuming she was dead he gently lifted Mrs. Todd's head when she gave a low moan which almost made the terrified

Hallgate, Cottingham.

26

man drop the head again. Instead he summoned the presence of mind to put the head gently down and leave the house to summon a constable and the doctor.

Doctor Galt of Cottingham had attended Mrs. Todd for the thirteen years she had been living in Hallgate and he was appalled by the state he found the house in. It had always been immaculate, well furnished and tidy.

Mrs. Todd's head had been battered with a heavy object, quite possibly the poker which was lying on the floor nearby. Her skull was severely fractured in such a way it could not have been caused by a fall. The doctor felt the wounds were about 12 hours old indicating they had been inflicted the previous night. The lady was treated and nursed at home by relatives.

Sergeant Jackson of the East Riding Constabulary took charge of the scene and found that the whole house had been ransacked and pots broken. He was surprised to find £8.10s.0d in gold in a small purse and a further 25s. wrapped in some paper. This find convinced the Sergeant that robbery could not have been the motive because there were 'plenty of things to have taken'!!

Mrs. Todd recovered sufficiently to move about and even to take small walks but always appeared to be in a semi-imbecile condition and was continually laughing in a high-pitched manner.

On one visit by the doctor Mrs. Todd had seemed a little more lucid and told him that a man and a woman had come to her house and the man had said 'I am going to do for you' and she remembered replying 'You had better not!' but after that her mind was blank.

On the 1st February 1901 Anne Todd died and the Coroner's Jury sitting in The Newington Hotel in Hull heard that her death had been due to natural causes by accelerated by her injuries. Because of the

THE HULL TIMES, FEBRUARY 9, 1901-

A COTTINGHAM TRAGEDY.

AGED LADY'S STRANGE VISITORS.

VERDICT OF "WILFUL MURDER."

News Headlands.

way in which she was beaten she had been given a cerebral condition which prevented her taking food. No further evidence was produced by police about whether there was blood on the poker, whether they had questioned relatives. Was there a man and woman who might have had connections with Mrs. Todd? Was she in dispute with anyone?

It may be they didn't realise they had a murder on their hands until it was too late. Suffice to say one old lady had been brutally murdered in the quiet little township of Cottingham and nobody seems to have taken much trouble to find and bring to justice the culprit(s).

Ten years previously the East Yorkshire Constabulary had been severely criticised for inefficiency in the case of the murder of Mary Jane Langley.

A person who attacks another and causes injuries may be charged with anything from 'causing actual bodily harm' to 'attempted murder', depending on the seriousness of the injuries and the reasons for the attack. If a person dies as the result of such injuries the crime is murder. But, they must die within one year and one day from the case coming to notice for a murder charge to be framed!!

The Coroner's Jury sitting at The Newington Hotel in Hull on Tuesday 6th February 1901 were only just able to bring in a verdict of 'Wilful Murder by some person or persons unknown'.

THREE HULL BUSINESSMEN

Between the beginnings of the two World Wars — 1914 — 1939 three bizarre murders took place in the City of Hull when three Hull businessmen were killed. None of the cases has ever been cleared up and no definite suspect emerged. Was a serial killer at large in the City?

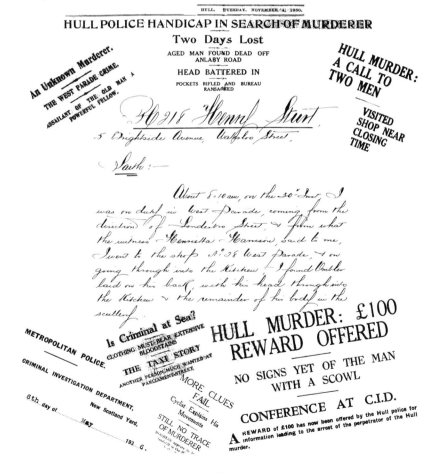

DAVID OMBLER

The Omblers were a well known family of retailers in the City of Hull. City Councillor Edwin, the eldest, was a wholesale stationer and David was a greengrocer trading from the shop at his home —28 West Parade, off the city's busy Anlaby Road.

On Saturday May 30th 1914, 70-year old David was up early as usual and made his way to the market at Humber Street to get his stock for the day. He felt tired because as usual he had not closed shop the night before until 10.45 pm and was beginning to feel his age. He was walking back home by 7.30 am and passed the time of day with William Muncastor in Londesborough Street.

On getting to his house Ombler prepared to make his breakfast. He still missed his late wife so very much and everything was much harder without her.

Henrietta Harrison, his cleaner, arrived at the house at 8 am as usual and immediately sensed something was wrong. She noticed ornaments knocked over and there was a funny smell.

When she entered the kitchen, to her horror, she found Mr. Ombler lying in a pool of blood on the floor, halfway between the kitchen and the scullery. The poker which was usually on the fender was lying by his side and broken into two pieces. The fire tongs were also nearby.

The cleaner rushed out to the nearby off-licene and stuttered her story to the owner Mrs. Stephenson. The two women quickly returned to Ombler's house, collecting Ethel Dibner. Mrs. Stephenson's

West Parade, off Anlaby Road.

servant on the way. Looking at the body closely, Mrs. Stephenson thought she detected a movement of the lips. She called for water and tried to pour some into the mouth of the wounded man. He appeared to be trying to speak but no discernible words came out.

Mrs. Harrison went out again and alerted a passing policeman —Constable Sturt, who informed his headquarters and arranged for Mr. Hartley, a Surgeon, to attend from his surgery in Spring Bank. Meanwhile Mr. Ombler remained semi-conscious and unable to speak. The doctor arranged for him to be removed to the Infirmary. At 10.55 am the same day he died without recovering consciousness.

Superintendent Kilvington took charge of the case which police viewed with even greater seriousness when it was realised that David Ombler was the brother of Councillor Edwin Ombler. Although such connections should not have affected the response, the facts of life in cities such as Hull at the time meant that relationships with those in positions of authority did carry considerable weight.

Intensive police activity started and almost the whole of Hull's CID was drafted on to what was in any case a most serious and brutal murder.

Initial police examination of the scene suggested that Mr. Ombler had been taken by surprise when he was attacked — his breakfast had been prepared but not eaten, the butter was warming on the fender and had not fully melted.

It appeared that robbery could have been a motive when it was discovered that Mr. Ombler's silver hunter watch together with a heavy silver curb albert from which hung a Soveriegn, together with a purse containing between £4 and £5, were all missing.

News of the murder spread quickly throughout the City and William Muncastor came forward to record his sighting of Mr. Ombler in the morning.

Information of a vital nature was also uncovered when Hannah Feetham and Ethel Dibner from Hunt's Terrace which overlooked Ombler's house related their experience. They were outside their homes at about 7.50 am, twenty minutes after the deceased had been seen walking home, when they both saw a man who was almost certainly the attacker. They saw the door of Ombler's shop open from the inside and a man came out, carefully closed the door behind him, pulled his cap down over his eyes and walked quickly away in the direction of Londesborough Street. They were able to provide a good description to the police.

Corp: Tel: No: 466.

W A N T E D in this C I T Y on SUSPICION of M U R D E R and
R O B B E R Y, about 7-30,a,m, to-day, 30th, May, 1914.
A MAN, name unknown, about 25 years of age, height 5ft 6 or 7 inches,
thin build, pale face, may have a slight dark moustache.
Dressed in a shabby dark ¾ overcoat, dark cloth cap, blue muffler
with white spots, rather dirty appearance.
The deceased named David Ombler, aged 70, kept a small shop & resided
alone at No: 28 West Parade, Hull.

About 7-40,a,m, a woman saw the above described man leave the
premises hurriedly & noticed him pull his cap over his eyes.

About 15 minutes later, the deceased was foundlying unconscious in
the back kitchen, his head having been battered by a fire poker &
pair of tongs.   He was conveyed to the Royal Infirmary where he
died about 11,a,m, never regaining consciousness.

A gent's silver lever hunter Watch, silver dial, metal hands,
silver curb albert & medal; a purse & probably about £4 or £5, in
money are missing & no doubt stolen.

Please cause diligent search and enquiry to be at once made at all
likely places within your district, and any information obtained
communicate to the undersigned.

G E O R G E M O R L E Y.

Chief Constable.
----

*Letter from George Morley – Chief Constable
regarding the death of David Ombler.*

This description of the suspect was circulated country-wide with a request that all ports be watched.

There was some suggestion that bad blood existed between Ombler and his son Thomas who lived at William Terrace, Woodstock Street. When interviewed by Superintendent Kilvington however, the son was able to prove he had still been at home until after 9 am on the day in question.

There was a history of mental instability on both sides of the Ombler family and some relatives had spent time in 'Willerby Asylum' but enquiries found that they could all be accounted for satisfactorily.

The public joined enthusiasticaly in the hunt for the killer, especially when a £50 reward was offered for information leading to an arrest. So enthusiastic was the flow of information that much police time was wasted in following up spurious leads.

Police attempted to follow up one lead by raiding a house in West Parade but were thwarted in their attempts to gain entry by the occupants' refusal to open the doors and by the large and noisy crowd which soon gathered to watch the proceedings. Eventually the officers withdrew to try at another and hopefully quieter time.

Not mentioned in the police reports at the time is the story told by Ombler's next door neighbour Mrs. Robson to the *Hull Daily Mail.* She recalled that at 11.30 pm on the evening before the murder, she had gone out into her backyard to fill the kettle. Hearing what she thought was a click, she looked up just in time to see a figure jumping off the wall dividing her house from the greengrocers'. Frightened 'out of her wits' she dropped the kettle and ran indoors. Peering through her curtains she saw a man in a three-quarters length coat, walking away in the direction of Spring Bank. She later found mud on the latch of her back gate indicating where the man had climbed over. She was convinced that the man she saw had been looking through Mr. Ombler's window.

Police continued their enquiries and many leads were followed up with no success. Various suggestions as to the identify of the offender were received but all the follow up investigations were unsuccessful. It was never clearly established whether the two men seen were one and the same but throughout the enquiry the investigating officers remained convinced the killing was the work of a local man. This may be borne out by the two similar killings which took place in the City in later years.

David Ombler,
Murdered.
30. 5. 14.

July   1914

Sir,

With reference to the
Murder of the person named in the
margin hereof.

It appears that he was
a widower, 73 years of age who
lived alone and carried on business
as a greengrocer at 28 West Parade
for about 30 years.

A woman named
Henrietta Harrison wife of George
Harrison 16 Sidney Terrace, Londesboro
St. was in the habit of going to his
shop every morning about 8 Am
to do his house work & Ombler
used to attend early morning
markets to buy his supplies for
his business &

About 7.30 Am on
the 30th May he was seen by William
Muncaster, 3 Wyndham Street in
Londesborough St. apparently
returning home from the market alone.

About 20 minutes later
a man, (see descriptive form attached)
was seen by Mrs Hannah Tusham,
10 Hunt Terrace, West Parade to
open Ombler's shop from the inside
and come into the street

The beginning of the police murder report.

34

The fact that the murderer was undoubtedly seen by the two women Feetham and Dibnah caused considerable frustration for investigators when they still could not clear the case up. Many of the Press thought that Scotland Yard should have been brought in to help but the chief constable, Mr. Morley, decided to stick with his own men. Whether or not the introduction of advice from 'The Yard' would have made any difference is difficult to say.

On 11th June an inquest jury brought in a verdict of 'murder by some person or persons unknown'.

The elderly David Ombler was laid to rest beside his wife in the cemetery at Spring Bank, a place he would have passed countless times on his journeys to and from the market. Over eighty years have passed since his death — perhaps the murderer shares the same resting place!!

SAMUEL SMITH

It was 1930, sixteen years after David Ombler met his death. Almost exactly one mile further away from the city centre than West Parade, but in the same Anlaby Road area of Hull, small, grey, bespectacled and rather nervous Sam Smith lived in his daughter Florence's house, recently built in Parkfield Drive, Hull. Living in the house with him were his daughter and son-in-law — Florence and Harold Wilson and their daughter Molly. For twenty-seven years Sam and his wife had kept a fish and chip shop in Woodcock Street and when he gave that up some years previously, he started a new business as a credit trader and money lender. His wife had died some years ago and it was her dying wish that the daughter take the old man in to live with her. Molly, the

69 Parkfield Drive, scene of the attack.

grand-daughter was well-known in the area as a music teacher.

Sam's sea-faring son-in-law got a job as captain of a ship based in Ireland which meant taking up residence there. His daughter stayed behind but decided that her bad nerves made it necessary to visit Ireland and spend a holiday with her husband for a few weeks. Reading between the lines it would appear that it was her father's presence in her home that was getting on her nerves.

As she told police on her return from Ireland, "My father was a very broody man — secretive. He used to sit in the house for hours and not speak. I wondered if he was comfortable but he said 'It was your mother's dying wish that I stopped with you and I shall carry it out!'" At the same time, grand-daughter Molly, not wishing to go with her parents, decided to leave the house and live in lodgings in Clyde Street.

Molly promised her mother she would keep an eye on Grandad Smith and usually visited him on a daily basis. As the first weekend in November approached, winter was really setting in and Molly saw the old man most days up until Thursday. Being busy she didn't visit again until Sunday when she found the house locked and presumed he was out for a walk which he did most Sundays.

Molly was engaged to a young Mr. Thompson and on Monday she asked him if he would check her grandad. Reaching No. 69 he was surprised to find it still locked. Knowing all the new houses were similar he borrowed a key from No. 71 and was easily able to open the front door.

Downstairs the house consisted of the kitchen and a small sitting room at the rear with a hallway and stairs plus the 'best' room at the front.

Rather nervously the young man entered the back kitchen and immediately saw Sam spread-eagled on the floor in the doorway between the back room and the hall. There was blood everywhere and the old man had obviously taken a severe beating to the head. His pockets had been pulled inside-out and a bootlace was tied tightly round his neck. The wireless was still going very quietly and sounded as if it needed a re-charged accumulator. It was later discovered that a gold watch and heavy double albert chain was missing from the house. Mrs. Wilson, the daughter, felt he could have had a lot of money. She grumbled that although he said he could not afford to pay her rent, he always seemed to have enough to go racing!

The Victim of the Outrage.

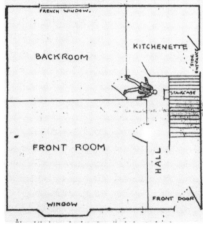

FRENCH WINDOW.

BACKROOM

KITCHENETTE

SIDE ENTRANCE

STAIRCASE

FRONT ROOM

HALL

WINDOW

FRONT DOOR

Samuel Smith,
and a plan of where he was found.

On finding the body the young man rushed from the house to inform the police and Detective Superintendent Reginald Howgate soon arrived to take charge.

The newly constructed Parkfield Drive was a quiet residential cul-de-sac off the Anlaby Road and the neighbourhood was very concerned when news of the murder spread. A number of passageways provided footpaths from Parkfield Drive to Wold Carr Road and Springfield Drive. The passages were dark and creepy at night and were known to be frequented by strange men who also congregated on the open space owned by the N.E. Railway at the bottom of Parkfield Drive.

Police concentrated their initial enquiries on trying to establish the old man's movements. His grand-daughter had seen him on the Thursday and a youth came forward and claimed to have seen Sam in the road between 5.50 pm and 6 pm on the Saturday. Mrs. Langley, his next door neighbour said that although he was quiet and kept very much to himself, she was sure she had heard him poking the fire between tea-time and bed-time on the Saturday.

The Superintendent was determined to clear this crime, especially when Chief Constable Howden arrived and reminded him that the force was still mystified by the death 16 years previously of David

38

Ombler, a similarly aged man and in similar circumstances! The local Watch Committee and the residents would expect results! For three days and nights the superintendent and his enquiry team worked non-stop. £150 reward was offered for information, a sum greater than the majority of Hull's population was earning in year.

Questions needed immediate answers!!
How did the murderer get access to the house?
What was the motive?
What weapon was used?

The medical examination indicated that the weapon had been hard and sharp. No blunt instrument was involved in this case!

Every day a crowd of morbid spectators gathered outside the house and to pass the time, read and re-read the notice giving details of Molly's music lessons. Two eight-year old boys playing in Springfield Way found a piece of wood with a nail sticking from it. Could this be the murder weapon? It was quickly sent off for examination to see if blood was present.

The house had been locked when the body was found and there was no sign of forcible entry. The keys to the side and back doors were found in their locks but there was no sign of the front door key. Did Mr. Smith know the murderer and let him in! Did the murderer find the door unlocked and take the old man by surprise? or, could it have been someone with access to a key from a neighbouring house which fitted. Young Mr. Thompson had found one from next door which had given access!!!

Of course money lending was not an entirely risk free business. Some very funny people could be involved in borrowing cash!! It was discovered that Sam still had over 200 clients owing him money on his books! A total of £400 was outstanding to him with £10 being the largest amount. It was the sort of business where enemies were easy to come by. Someone being pressurised to repay? Someone refused a loan?

But perhaps more to the point rumours may well have been circulating that he kept large amounts of cash at his home. Despite his daughter's grumbles he was well known to have kept a fairly hefty size roll of bank notes in his hip pocket and there was no trace of this.

The missing watch was easily recognisble being 10 years old and with the initials SHS engraved on the inside. Posters with a drawing of the watch and publicising the reward were circulated around the city.

A piece of crumpled brown paper with bloodstains on it was found in the house near to the body which, from its creases appeared to have been wrapped around the piece of wood found by the boys. So had the murderer come prepared to attack the old man, carrying the weapon wrapped like a parcel and suddenly, when confronted, hit him with it?

A further twist to the mystery had come to light when Mrs. Wilson returned to Hull. She produced a letter received from her father giving news from home. The letter had been written and signed by Samuel but the envelope was in someone else's hand! Whose??

Another strange incident occurred when a man reported finding a black felt hat with initials T.W. in the passage between Parkfield Drive and Wold Carr Lane at about 11 am on the Sunday morning after the murder. It belonged to Samuel's son-in-law and had been in a wardrobe in the house. The hat was bone dry despite heavy rain on Saturday night/Sunday morning!!!

Samuel had been sighted early Saturday evening and had been heard raking the fire later in the evening. The murder was most likely to have occurred between late Saturday night and Sunday morning. But the hat threw all this into confusion. Perhaps someone had been trying to lay a false trail?

It appeared from blood marks on the towel in the kitchen that the intruder had washed his hands before leaving. No lights were on which meant either it was daylight when the attack took place or, the murderer had very carefully switched everything off before he left!!

Another witness came forward to say that lights were on in the house at 11 pm on the Saturday which supported the neighbour's evidence about poking the fire!

Perhaps the most significant piece of evidence was provided by Lizzie Parker of 61 Parkfield Drive. Amazingly she had not been seen during the extensive police enquiries in the neighbourhood. She related how, at about 11.10 on on the night of the murder she had seen a man near Smith's house. He was fairly tall and she saw him leave the front door and walk down the side passage towards the back of the house. The person was never traced and would appear to be the most likely one to have been Smith's murderer. An amazingly similar sighting to that made in the Ombler case!

One week after being found the body of Samuel Henry Smith

HULL CITY POLICE.

Criminal Investigation Department,
Alfred Gelder Street,
6th November, 1930.

MURDER.
£150 REWARD

On the 3rd November, 1930, the body of one **Samuel Henry Smith** was found in his home, 69, **Parkfield Drive**, in this City, death having been caused by blows from some blunt instrument, inflicted by some person or persons unknown.

The deceased was last seen alive about 6-0 p.m. on the 1st November, 1930.

Information is now urgently sought respecting the following articles which are known to have been in his possession just prior to the murder:

1st. Gent's gold watch, keyless, white dial, English numerals, black hands, second hand missing, glass may also be missing, initials S.H.S. inscribed on back case, believed on outside; this watch is about 25 years old and fairly heavy.

2nd. Gent's gold double albert, curb pattern, bar in centre with drop chain and a Queen Victoria Jubilee sovereign as pendant, fastened in a gold ring with a split screw.

At the time when the body was found a mohair boot lace was found to be tied around the neck.

The above reward is offered to any person who will give information leading to the arrest and conviction of the murderer.

THOMAS E. HOWDEN,
Chief Constable.

A REPRODUCTION of the notice issued by the Hull police in connection with the Parkfield-drive murder.

Article in the 'Hull Daily Mail' regarding the murder.

41

was interred in Hull's Northern Cemetery.

Although many leads continued to come to light which police vigorously followed up, it was to no avail. No real suspect has come to light to this day!

Who was stalking the streets of Hull? First elderly David Ombler and now Samuel Smith. Who next???

OSWALD FISHER WALKER

Only six years after the murder of Sam Smith detectives in the city of Hull were faced with another serious case in March 1936, at a time when the world news was full of the threat being posed by Nazi Germany.

Oswald Fisher Walker was 70 years old, a native of Sheffield who had come to Hull 35-40 years previously and set up a business as a tool merchant, initially in Lime Street. He lived in Anlaby Common until 1932 when his wife died. Two years later he married Miss Warwick, an elderly resident of Cliff Road in Hornsea and went to live with her on the coast.

He was a strict Methodist and despite his age continued in full time work, travelling to and from his place of business by train. His business had now been moved to George Street in Hull for many years.

He was described in the Press at the time as a jolly white-haired old man who didn't seem to have a care in the world. He was hard working, amiable and kindly. Police enquiries however, were later to discover a somewhat different picture. Walker had a reputation within his family of being somewhat eccentric and very mean. While he was very generous in his dealings with the Church, he was also very secretive and none of his relatives knew anything about his financial position.

He usually arrived home in Hornsea at around 7 pm. On the day of the murder he told his wife he would be later home so she hadn't worried when he didn't turn up as usual. When however the time for the last train had passed she had become very worried and contacted her daughter, Mrs. Ethel Pattinson, who lived in Hull. Mr. Pattinson contacted Walker's son Norman, who also lived in Hull and the two men met and went to the George Street shop. Finding the place locked and apparently in darkness at about 12 midnight they went to Worship Street Police Station to express their concern.

Constable Winterbottam returned to the shop with them and Norman Walker decided to break into the premises. The Constable returned to Worship Street and returned with a colleague who was a

Interior part of the George Street shop.

police fireman, and a crowbar. A quick search of the rambling building confirmed their worst fears when the body of Oswald Walker was found lying, battered to death on the floor of a landing leading to a lower sales area. There was a severe wound visible to the head.

The shop had a double frontage on to George Street, and behind was a long narrow workshop at the end of which was a flight of six stairs leading down to a door opening onto New Garden Street which ran parallel with George Street. Another door on the left of the long workshop and about halfway along it, opened on to a landing leading to another large sales area. It was on this landing that the body was found, fully dressed, even to an overcoat but with no hat.

Dr. John Cumming the police surgeon was quickly on the scene and pronounced life extinct. He expressed surprise that despite the severity of the wounds and the amount of blood which had seeped through the landing floor, there were none of the usual splashes on neighbouring walls and other nearby objects. It appeared the old man had been taken by surprise by his attacker, seized from behind by a hand placed in the back of his collar which partly asphyxiated him and then struck repeatedly on the head. Broken spectacles and dentures were nearby and his pipe was at his side, a sure indication of the sudden and unexpected nature of the attack.

Chief Constable Howden, Chief Superintendent Smith the deputy chief constable and Detective Superintendent Mulchinock were quickly on the scene and the Chief Constable, fearful of another undetected murder, sent an urgent telephone message to the Assistant Commissioner Crime at Scotland Yard at 4.45 am and asked for assistance. Five hours later Chief Inspector John Sands, one of the Yard's Big Five with his assistant Sergeant Griffin and fingerprint expert Inspector Fred Cherry were leaving Kings Cross station for Hull. Fred Cherry was in later years to become the world's foremost fingerprint expert. They arrived in the early afternoon and wasted no time in visiting the premises in George Street where they spent the rest of the day. The sensational happening had by now attracted considerable crowds who stood outside watching events. Police attempts to move them away were resisted good naturedly.

A comprehensive search of the scene revealed little of help. The only possible clue being a part patterned footprint on the bottom of the steps where Mr. Walker had been found. The man had been battered with a blunt instrument but this was never discovered. As Inspector Sands said at the time. "the premises contained thousands of items which could possibly have been used".

Time of death was fixed at between 8 pm and 9 pm on the previous evening and efforts were directed towards finding a motive for the murder. Mr. Walker was known to carry two wallets, a business one and a personal one. The latter would normally have had about £20 in it. This wallet was missing but while robbery might have been the motive it was strange that the second, business wallet was still on the body as was a heavy gold watch and chain, clearly visble.

Initially suspicion fell on Walker's son Norman and this was

This is Mr Walker: Did You See Him Last Thursday?

Oswald Fisher Walker.

strengthened by the fact that when he, his brother-in-law and the two policemen had found his father's body, he was the only one who would not look at it.

Until July 1935 Norman had worked for his father at a weekly £7 wage and had been in charge of a branch of the business selling vehicles and heavy machinery at a depot at Anlaby. Norman was more pushy and tried to get his father to adopt more aggressive business tactics. The old man always rejected Norman's suggestions so the young man did deals on his own and pocketed the money. This infuriated the father who sacked him and sold the Anlanby Yard.

Norman, not to be beaten, set up in opposition to his father from Silvester Street, not far away and soon secured nearly two-thirds of his father's business. Norman did not visit his father's George Street premises from the time he was sacked until the body was found. Despite this, business relations between the two had become quite amicable and they bought things from one another.

Chief Inspector Sands followed this up and persuaded solicitors acting for the dead man to show him the will. Suspicions were confirmed when it was found there were three wills, the earliest splitting Walker's estate between his son and daughter with the last one giving everything to the girl and leaving the boy only the watch and chain which had been found with the body.

Eventually the Yard team pulled Norman Walker in for questioning. After a lengthy examination however Chief Inspector Sands wrote 'I am satisfied that Norman Walker is in no way connected with the crime!'

The other main line of enquiry which developed centred on a mystery customer. It appeared Mr. Walker had stayed late in the shop on the Wednesday prior to the murder and had mentioned to a number of people that a man had been interested in a saw bench. Staff got the impression that the man was returning to the shop on the Friday evening to pursue the purchase and Mr. Walker was muttering about the difficulty of getting country folk to part with their money. He also mentioned that the man could not get to the shop early because he had to get from Beverley where he worked!

William Davies a 20-year old shop assistant at the tool merchants remembered a man coming to the shop one evening and having long discussions with Walker about a saw bench and on leaving saying "I'll see you again"! He described the man as in his mid thirties with a scowling face and wearing rather dirty grey clothing. This man became a major suspect with the assistant Davies as the only person who could identify him.

There is little doubt Walker was expecting to sell a saw bench on the Friday evening he was murdered because he sent his errand boy out during the day to get some parts to repair it.

On Friday afternoon he gave Davies a slip of paper to take to Miss Walker his clerk, to type an account. As he did so he said "It's for £30.5s.6d and if he buys the lot (meaning the saw-bench and countershaft) I shall give him back the 5/6d" No name was mentioned. Miss Walker placed the typed invoice in an envelope and put it on the corner of Walker's desk. It was never found again!

Appeals in the Press and by way of posters resulted in many people coming forward with information about the case. One of these was Joseph Lorrimar, a Corporation bus driver. He had been driving his bus in George Street in the early evening the murder was committed and saw a man standing well back on the pavement on the opposite side of the street to the tool shop. The man was staring intently at Walker's shop, so much so the bus driver looked across the road to see what he was looking at. When he re-passed the shop an hour-and-a-half later the man was still there. Police felt the description given was similar to the saw bench suspect and that maybe he was watching for all the staff to leave before going into the shop.

A Mr. Webster passed the shop at 8.25 pm, and noticed a bright light in the shop but that the windows were not lighted. He saw two men standing inside and from his description one was obviously Walker. The other man vaguely fitted the description of the suspect and was no doubt the murderer.

A week went by and little or no progress was being made. Press interest was intense both locally and nationally and the national *Daily Express* retained a retired West Yorkshire chief inspector to comment on the case. Ex Detective Inspector Bates who had personally solved four murders was of the opinion the crime had been commited by 'a master criminal after lengthy planning which marked him out as a genius among criminals!!'

Whatever the situation Chief Constable Howden was beginning to get concerned. Although well known and well liked in the City he knew that even his best friends on the Watch Committee would be getting restless if this case was not cleared.

A conference was held with all the officers working on the investigation attending. Chief Inspector Sands lent some credence to Mr. Bates' views by saying he felt the attack was pre-meditated and well planned. He thought the attacker was probably known to his victim and that he had been allowed into the shop without suspicion. The fact that he had apparently left the premises by a side door into New Garden Street indicated he was either reasonably familiar with the shop or had forced his elderly victim to reveal the door's whereabouts. The key to the door had usually been kept on the inside of the lock but was missing after the murder!

As is usual with murders of a senseational nature rumours were abounding in Hull with arrests being made daily in different parts of the country.

In fact the reality was quite different as the officers attending the conference knew. Where and who was the man with the scowl? Could there have been more than one person involved? The head injuries indicated Mr. Walker had been struck sideways — perhaps one man had got his hand down the victim's collar to restrain him while the other one struck him with whatever weapon was used. Ideas flowed round the room as the meeting went on. This sort of general discussion with everyone involved in the enquiry was new to the Hull men but despite their determined efforts they were forced to admit they were no nearer the truth!

Routine enquiries had eliminated all possible visitors to the shop except for the man with the scowl. Reports of people who were said to have stayed in the city at the time were being checked. A week had gone by but there was no real progress.

A few days after the conference another and perhaps most significant development in the enquiry came to notice. Information was received from the Fruit Market that the driver of a red lorry from Nottingham was understood to have said that he had left Hull between 12 mn and 2 am on the Saturday morning that the body had been found, with a load of potatoes. On the outskirts of the city he had picked up a male hitch-hiker and dropped him off at Doncaster at about 4 am.

More significantly, soon after leaving Hull the man had pulled a fold-over type wallet from his pocket which sounded similar to the one missing from the murder scene. He had opened the window of the vehicle and thrown the wallet into the roadside or over the hedge — the driver could not be sure.

THE
POLICE GAZETTE
PUBLISHED BY AUTHORITY.

NEW SERIES.　　　WEDNESDAY, MARCH 18, 1936.　　　No. 67, VOL. XXIII.

All communications for insertion in the POLICE GAZETTE and Supplement B should be addressed to THE COMMISSIONER OF POLICE OF THE METROPOLIS, NEW SCOTLAND YARD, LONDON, S.W.1, and the envelope marked " **C.R.O. (Police Gazette)** " in the top left hand corner.

Communications for insertion in the Supplement C (Aliens) and the Deserters List should be addressed as directed thereon.

PHILIP GAME,

The Commissioner of Police of the Metropolis.

Murder.

1.—Yorkshire (E.R.), Hull (City).—About 12.35 a.m. 14th inst., Oswald Fisher Walker, who carried on business of a tool maker at 29–31, George Street, Hull, was found dead. He had apparently been preparing to leave for the night.

His head had been badly battered with a blunt instrument and it would appear that a pointed instrument had also been used.

The murderer apparently left the premises by a door which was found to be locked, but the key which had been left on the inside of the lock was missing.

A number of Bank of England £1 or 10s. notes, miscellaneous correspondence, a driving licence in name of Oswald Fisher Walker, also 2 photographs (postcard size) (one of deceased and wife, and another of a family group), are missing, these are believed to have been contained in a brown leather pocket wallet.

The below-described **MAN** is suspected : B. 1899 or 1900, 5ft. 8in., medium build, c. and h. dk., clean shaven, round chin, round face, slightly scowling, unkempt dirty hands ; dress, working class clothing (dk. colour), dirty grey cap, believed also wearing dirty mackintosh with belt.

This man called at the deceased's premises and made enquiries as to a saw bench, which Mr. Walker had for sale, and which was stored in close proximity to where the body was found.

It was said by the deceased that the man who visited him on 7th and 11th inst. was again calling on 13th inst., after business hours, to complete the transaction.

The saw bench is of the type that could be used for cutting logs and the deceased has said that it was a firewood dealer that was negotiating the business, but the story may have been a ruse to lure the deceased to the rear of the premises after the employees had left for the night.

Copy of Police Gazette recording the murder of Oswald Fisher Walker

Who was this driver and more importantly, who was his passenger? Was it the man with the scowl or someone completely different? Was he the murderer? It may have been just another rumour but no chances could be taken. Urgent messages were sent to Nottingham and Doncaster and the busy fruit market became the centre of police enquiries.

Still enquiries dragged on with no results. Chief Inspector Sands and Sergeant Griffin worked for another month and travelled all over the country following leads. They visited the Midlands, London and South Wales. The reward offered for information was increased from £100 to £250 — all to no avail.

Then, in April, dramatic news arrived from Tettenhall Police in Staffordshire. They had arrested a 29-year old known criminal James Burson on fraud and theft charges and he had admitted murdering Mr. Walker. He was known to have visited Hull on a number of occasions!

On the 21st April Inspector Sands and Sergeant Griffin interviewed Burson at Birmingham's Winson Green Prison. They were aware that he had previous convictions for theft and false pretences. The man appeared quite rational and after being cautioned made a fourteen page statement in two parts.

Burson opened by saying he had to tell the truth. His story started when he got a lift on a lorry from the Midlands to Grimsby and then to Hull where he tried to get work on the docks. He got bed and breakfast in George Street for two shillings and sixpence the first night and then slept on lorries which pulled up for the night at a café just outside the city.

He went on "I had a cosh when I left Wolverhampton. I bought it off a chap in the cattle market on Saturday 29th February. I gave him one-and-sixpence and three packets of Woodbines for it."

Burson mentioned two visits to Walker's shop, the first to buy a chisel and on the second "there was somebody else in the shop helping him (Walker), a young man who looked like an assistant. That is what made me start to talk about a saw then. I had nothing and intended to try and get something out of him then but the young man being there made me start guessing. I started talking about a saw for sawing firewood and told him that another fellow and me were thinking about buying a saw for sawing firewood... he told me that he had got a saw bench that would suit us."

He went on to describe how Walker insisted on showing him a

circular saw in a back room. He said he left the shop and after going for a cup of tea he returned and finding the premises locked, forced his way in to search for money. He had seen Walker put sixpence in a jar when he had bought the chisel.

"...the old man must have heard me moving about because he came downstairs. He put the light on and then he recognised me."

He then described how his victim had apparently just got out of bed by the way he was dressed and went on to detail the murder and how he ran away after the killing.

He described a wallet he stole and said he hitched a lift on a lorry and threw it, minus the contents, out of the lorry into a field near Doncaster. The statement continued with a long detailed description of his movements since leaving Hull.

The two detectives were extremely sceptical about the truth of the statement particularly as Burson had so many details of the shop layout and Mr. Walker's actions so obviously wrong. Nevertheless they invited him to sign it and to their surprise he burst into tears and said he had not been telling the truth.

He started a second statement, "I have not told you everything, it's no good me saying I have because I haven't. I suppose the Assistant will know me again. I know I've not given you the proper lay out of the shop. I'm afraid to do so as I'll implicate somebody else. I'll get somebody else into it besides myself. I won't squeal on him. I've squealed on myself. I did it and I'll take the responsibility. I'm not going to drag him into it.

I did it after closing hours, not midnight and no so long after shop hours. You can't say what I've told you is untruth, barring time and the description and the lay of it. We planned to force our way in. There were two of us but I shan't squeal on him. He'll see I'm in trouble and he'll help me out on Thursday. It were arranged to be done. The old man did not come downstairs or anything of that. He was waiting for us. There were only him there...."

Burson continued on about how they had arranged to visit the shop to see a saw and they were looking at the saw and "...he (the accomplice) got hold of him by the collar, his right hand was on his collar on the right side of his neck and he had got hold of the old man's left wrist and had pulled it back. I was on his left side and struck the old man on the back of his head three times..." He said he left the shop, leaving his mate behind and they arranged to meet in the nearby fish and chip shop. He claimed the rest of his story as told the first time was true.

Chief Inspector Sands felt that the second version was much nearer to the facts as they knew them but Burson refused absolutely to name his alleged confederate. He did say he met him while in Birmingham prison in 1935 but despite strenuous efforts, the prison governor was unable to identify the person. It was doubted if the person ever existed.

The Chief Inspector, in his report on the case, concluded that Burson had either (1) committed the murder alone or with someone else, (2) had had the true facts communicated to him by the person responsible or (3) had read local newspapers and read between the lines in such a way as to practically reconstruct the crime with some degree of accuracy but Burson maintained he had not seen a newspaper since the murder. The Inspector does not mention whether or not the simple test suggested by Burson himself was ever made. Was he put on an identification parade to see if Mr. Walker's Assistant recognised him?

Burson also said he met his alleged confederate in Manchester on 11th April 1936 when the latter had showed him about £20 in cash and a revolver, which was stated to be proceeds of a case of office-breaking near Manchester Police Station. Subsequent enquiries revealed such a case did occur and that cash and a revolver were stolen.

The detectives returned to Wolverhampton and re-interviewed Burson after he had appeared at Court. They were joined on this occasion by Superintendent Mulchinock of Hull in view of the importance of the situation.

Burson was a completely different man! He was obviously suffering from severe mental stress and little of sense could be gleaned from him. He said his confederate had been named Owen. A Harold Owen had been in prison with Burson in 1935 but it was quickly established that this man was serving a prison sentence in Birmingham at the time of Walker's murder.

It was felt Burson was cleverly mixing fact and fiction in his alleged admission and as there was absolutely no corroboration of his story, it was not pursued further. Perhaps it should have been.

Burson subsequently wrote three letters from prison to his mother, wife, and Chief Constable of Hull, all admitting complicity in Walker's murder. In his letter to the Chief Constable he named his accomplice as Owen Wainwright. Enquiries failed to find such a man.

53

A Jury was empanelled for the resumed Inquest on Oswald Fisher Walker on 13th May 1936. The Coroner was in possession of a thirty page report on the investigation from Scotland Yard which he felt it inappropriate to read to the Court. Instead he confined himself to saying there was no doubt in his mind that the police investigation had been most thorough. The Jury could be satisfied that Mr. Walker had been murdered and the Coroner concluded by asking them to return a verdict of 'murder by some person or persons unknown'. Over one thousand statements had been taken in the course of the enquiry!

In fact many questions were left unanswered when the Scotland Yard detectives returned to London for good after the Walker investigation. Was there only one person involved? Was it the scowling man? Was it the hitch hiker? Were they one and the same person? Perhaps most importantly, had the police been very near to solving the crime with the man Burson?

Whoever it was — could it have been the same person responsible for David Ombler's death in 1914 and Sam Smith's in 1930. Burson wasn't old enough to have done all three. It may seem a long period between the cases but, they were very similar. A serial killer could have been born in 1894, been 20 years old when David Ombler died; 36-years old when Sam Smith was killed, and only 6 years older in 1936. Perfectly feasible and he may have continued to live in Hull for many years afterwards!!!

MISSING IN SUSPICIOUS CIRCUMSTANCES

There can be no greater frustration for an investigator to be unsure whether a person has been murdered or not. Someone vanishes, no body is found!! The following cases from this area have tantalised the police for years.

'I shall not give up hoping'

She could not disappear without trace

Police launch big probe after 18-month silence

Gloria: Pub rugby team to be quizzed

All the leads fizzle out in frustration

FREDERICK OLIVER WILKINSON

Sixty-one year old Frederick Oliver Wilkinson was a self employed coalman who lived quietly with his wife Maude at 1 Durham Street, off Holderness Road in Hull. A teetotaller and man of routine habits he took his lorry each morning to his yard in Newbridge Road and loaded it up. When he had finished for the day his only interest was to go home and get washed, fed and sat down to watch television. He didn't mix much and had no connections with crime as far as was known.

All that changed on Wednesday 11th January 1961. Wilkinson left home as usual but failed to return at the end of the day. Enquiries soon revealed that his lorry was parked unattended in Albion Street in the City centre and that it had been there at least since 3.30 pm.

Police were puzzled but initially not over anxious. People did go missing in bizarre circumstances and were often accounted for after a short time. But there were unusual features here. A coalman, dressed in obvious working clothes of a corduroy cap, black jacket and waistcoat, the latter with silver buttons, brown trousers, black boots and a brown scarf, would tend to make him slightly conspicuous.

Routine enquiries with Wilkinson's customers revealed nothing of interest at all. He had seemed in normal health and temper when he had been delivering that morning.

Then suddenly the tempo of the case quickened and suspicions began to harden. It was discovered that on the day Wilkinson vanished, 40-years old Bernard Richardson, known as Mick, an ex lodger at the Wilkinsons' home, had vanished too! Was this coincidence or was there something more sinister behind this?

It transpired that Richardson, a married man, had formed an association with Fred Wilkinson's twenty-four year old daughter Patricia, while staying at her parents' home and she had been cited in divorce proceedings between Richardson and his wife.

Although over sixty, Fred Wilkinson was no weakling. Broad shoulders and well developed muscles revealed his lifelong trade of heaving coal and made him a very strong man. Despite being an inveterate smoker and suffering a minor heart attack a year previously he still handled heavy work with ease.

Detectives were now moving onto the case and Detective Inspector Ken Ogram, later to become Chief Constable of the British Transport Police was put in day-to-day charge, under the overall supervision of head of CID Jim Cocksworth.

With no sign of the coalman, interest tended to centre on the missing Mick Richardson. Could he be responsible for Wilkinson's disappearance? If so, what was the motive? Police were trying to solve two baffling vanishing acts which might or might not be connected.

By the Wednesday following the two men's abrupt disappearances a full scale police operation was in motion to trace either or both men. Wilkinson's last deliveries had been traced to the Newbridge Road area and the Albion Street car park attendant confirmed his lorry had been parked there about 3.30 pm. Richardson had also been seen in the area at about that time.

Reports that Richardson had been seen in the Crown and Humber Tavern pubs in the Paull area at lunch time on the day of the mystery led to massive police searches of woodland and fields , using tracker dogs. Some reports even said he was driving a coal lorry at the time.

But rumours were already becoming rife. Further sightings of the same man were reported from Beverley on the days after the two vanished. As police said at the tinme, 'He (Richardson) must have known we were looking for him!'

Further enquiries were made at Sutton where Richardson was alleged to have slept rough on occasions, sometimes using the local Scout hut. He was thought to have slept at his ex-wife's house on a number of occasions, often without her knowledge.

With the Paull lead being the most definite in a baffling mystery, police were cautious about overlooking anything and enlisted the help of the local Territorial Army to assist in the search. But all was to no avail.

Then the breakthrough! On Tuesday, almost a fortnight after the disappearance of Wilkinson, a phone call was received to say that Mick Richardson was staying in a house at Rosedale Grove, off Spring Bank West. He was arrested and charged in respect of some non-payment of fines warrant, which allowed police to keep him in

Frederick Wilson.   *Det.-Supt. James Cocksworth.*

custody. While in the station overnight he slipped and slightly injured himself and had to be removed to the Infirmary. Everyone was sure the mystery would now be cleared up!

Days and weeks went by, Richardson hobbled into the Hull Magistrates Court and received a six-week sentence for his non-payment of fines. Later the same year he appeared again, this time charged with obtaining clothes by false pretences. It was then revealed police had seized all his clothing for forensic tests!

Since then there have been no developments and police have always remained tight-lipped about the case. Nothing has been said about the reasons for Richardson going missing, or about the fate of coalman Wilkinson. Police enquiries went on for many months afterwards but with no apparent result.

The probability is that either it was pure coincidence the two men went missing together and that Richardson's reason was a simple one or, more likely, that Richardson was in some way involved in his landlord's disappearance but police could prove no criminal act on his part.

There has been no inquest on Frederick Wilkinson — there has never been a body! The case is still recorded as a simple missing person but the signs must be ominous.

In 1977 Jim Cocksworth by now deputy chief constable of Humberside, retired and mused on his departure "the failure to clear the mystery of Fred Wilkinson's disappearance satisfactorily has been one of the greatest disappointments of my career."

FREDERICK DEAN

Frederick Dean lived at 43 Franklin Street, off Holderness Road in Hull. He was 15 years old, slim and with fair curly hair. The young man walked with a pronounced limp, dragging his right foot. He was spastic.

He was an only son and always looked forward to a family Christmas. It was 1963 and he was at home with his mother, who was busy cooking the Christmas dinner. Frederick left the house saying he was going to take his presents to show to his grandmother. That was the last time either his mother or his father saw him. No trace of the boy or his body was ever found.

Superintendent Ron Joyce, head of the police division immediately took charge of the investigation and a description was circulated. He had been wearing a brown suede sheepskin lined jacket with a fur collar, a grey single breasted suit, white shirt, red tie and black pointed buckle shoes.

43 Franklin Street.

Friends and neighbours led by the boy's father — Frederick (senior) started to search the neighbourhood. At first it was thought he might have gone to the Estuary foreshore. Reports of alleged sighting began to come in from all parts including a suggestion he had been seen on the evening of Boxing Day on Hedon Road, near to Earle's Road. It was said he had been walking towards the city boundary.

During the course of the search by civilian friends and relatives, the distraught father collapsed through exhaustion.

No-one knows to this day what happened to young Frederick, a tragic mystery which is unlikely ever to be solved. Without finding any trace of him or his body the task was an impossible one for the police. Was he murdered? Did he drown in the estuary? Christmas never came again to the Dean household.

One unconfirmed report claimed the boy's name appeared in the diaries of the notorious Brady and Hindley!

GLORIA BIELBY

She was stunning! In 1979 blonde, gregarious, fun-loving, and beautiful 34-years old Gloria Bielby lived with her husband Bernard and 11-years old son Nigel in quiet Dawnay Road, Bilton, on the eastern outskirts of Hull. Bernard had bought a butcher's business after being made redundant from Imperial Typewriters, their son was at a Preparatory School in Bridlington and Gloria, an ex model, worked as a Secretary at Reckitt & Coleman's offices in the city.

The domestic situation was a strange one as both had decided to go their own ways within the marriage. Bernard preferred work and the quiet home life whereas Gloria loved the social whirl and the friendship of other men. Bernard claimed to be aware of her life style and not to bother about it. They had lived together in a travesty of a marriage for the previous five years for the sake of their son and had used separate bedrooms before that. He had a good idea she was carrying on with a married man.

Recently they had finally decided to separate and Bernard offered his wife £3,000 in cash to buy a new car as part of a separation

Dawnay Road, Bilton.

settlement. He had been saving hard and done good business over Christmas thus allowing this generous gesture. Gloria had decided to buy a second-hand Ford Capri from a local dealer. These facts were to be confirmed by subsequent police enquiries.

Thirty-nine year old Mike Blackburn, a good looking vending machine salesman and amateur rugby league player, considered he had been Gloria's regular boyfriend for at least seven years and *this* intriguing story begins when he dropped her off outside her twin sister's home, at about 9.30 pm on a freezing cold Thursday evening, the 1st February 1979.

Reckitts, where Gloria worked had been closed due to some industrial problems that day and so Gloria and Mike

Gloria Bielby.

had spent the time in the Driffield and Bridlington area. Gloria's brother-in-law walked her home that night because she had been receiving nuisance phone calls which had frightened her. Bernard, her husband remembers her arriving home and said it was then he gave her the £3,000 to get the car.

Bernard's alarm went off at 6 am the next morning and shortly afterwards he heard Gloria leave the house. He was not very surprised as his wife seldom informed him of her plans but, when he couldn't find the hair dryer he wondered if she'd gone away for a time! She had stayed away for days at a time previously and although she always blamed work commitments he had a good idea she had been with the boyfriend. The thought did cross his mind that she might have left him for good this time!

Mike Blackburn became very puzzled about Gloria's whereabouts on the fateful Friday. He rang her office in the afternoon expecting to make arrangements to take her to collect her new car and to his surprise was told she had not been in to work that day. He could get no answer from her home.

Gloria's parents first became aware of her disappearance on the Saturday. Her mother was waiting for Gloria to come and pick her up, as had been arranged, when without warning Bernard rang to say she had apparently left home.

Even stranger, she had mentioned no plans to anyone, husband, parents, son, boyfriend, none of them had any inkling she was going and this was most unlike Gloria!! She would have mentioned some plans even if they had been lies!

Bernard discovered she had taken quite a few clothes and other personal things with her but didn't think this very significant in view of her previous unannounced 'trips'.

Initially no great fuss was made over the woman's disappearance, her husband presumed she would turn up like some bad penny and in view of his attitude and rumours rife about her life style, everyone seemed to think she had just left home and gone to live elsewhere, presumably with someone else! Police tended to agree with this view. After all, thousands of women walk out on their domestic

Bernard Bielby.

64

arrangement every day!

It was not until many months had gone by they became more interested as rumours began to grow. People, particularly Gloria's parents Mr. and Mrs. Thompson, began to worry because they felt sure their daughter would have tried to get in touch with them, at least to let them know all was well. Coincidentally Mr. Thompson worked as a civilian at police headquarters and he let his suspicions be known. Experienced Detective Superintendent Bob Carmichael personally took over the investigation and formed a team of detectives to help him.

His enquiries soon uncovered a very strange and quite inexplicable set of circumstances!

Det. Supt. Bob Carmichael.

Reckitts, the large Company where she worked was most cooperative in the enquiry and allowed over 600 questionnaires to be completed by their employees. The results of these and other enquiries showed that between July — August 1978 Gloria had been regularly picked up outside her workplace at lunch times by a man in a red Morris car. His description did not tally with that of Mike Blackburn and to this day it has never been discovered who this man was.

Robert and Elsie Pauling lived next door to the Bielbys and Mrs. Pauling, when seen by the police team claimed she had seen Gloria loading cases into a red Ford Escort car at about 11 am on the morning she disappeared. She said she could fix the time and day by the fact that she always cleaned her windows on Friday mornings and the next day Mr. Bielby told her Gloria was missing. The car was being driven by a man described as about 40 years, grey hair, slim build and about 5»9" tall. He was well dressed. Mrs. Pauling's evidence was treated with some care by police in view of her age but she was adamant about her facts. She knew Michael Blackburn and had seen him there regularly but was certain this was a different man but that he also had been a regular caller at the house, two or three times each week in January, so regular in fact the Paulings had nick-named him Dapper-Dan! But who was this man? He did not fit the decription of either Mike Blackburn or the man alleged to have picked her up at lunchtime outside Reckitts! The latter was supposed to have dark hair!!

The witness made a photo-fit of Dapper-Dan which was circulated nationwide but with no results.

Once the investigation was under way the police team naturally homed in on the two obvious suspects, husband and boyfriend. Both were subjected to intense questioning and for days the house and gardens at Dawnay Road were systematically examined by trained staff. Blackburn claimed that at one stage he was being interviewed three or four times each week, on one occasion for over seven hours. In the end Superintendent Carmichael felt as satisfied as he could be that the two men were not involved. He says now, nearly twenty years after the event, that he feels easy about both men.

An artist's impression of the "third man".

So, what could have happened to Gloria Bielby? Who else could have been involved? She was unlikely to have gone away alone and with nowhere to go, she was not like that! Was it one of the mysterious strangers seen at her workplace and at her home? Was Mrs. Pauling right about her sighting? Were the two men one and the same? The mystery deepened!!!

As the story broke the Press had field days with sensational headlines and articles. This massive resultant publicity fuelled more and more rumous and speculation. The police on the case were kept extremely busy

66

following up leads both genuine and fictitious.

Gloria was extremely well known in local rugby club circles and strong suspicions became centred on a party of rugby players who had gone from the York area to Munchen Gladbach in Germany at about the time of Gloria's disappearance. It was suggested she may have even gone with them on their tour. All the group were seen and although knowing Gloria well, they could not be connected in any way with her disappearance.

Excitement was caused by information received that a body had been buried in a Hessle garden but despite the deployment of body sniffing dogs, no trace was found.

In October 1980 a witness was found who recalled a man picking Gloria up outside Reckitts in a red Ford Escort. The man was described as being about 35-years old, 5'10" tall, athletic build with thick dark brown hair. He looked slightly Jewish and very much the young Executive type. The two had also been seen embracing in the Prospect Centre. according to the same witness. This sighting, if genuine, tied in much closer with that of the man who was seen picking Gloria up outside her home.

At the same time a number of people rang in to say they thought they had seen Gloria acting in an episode of ITV's 'The Professionals' which was coincidentally named 'The Fugitive'. Officers were sent to the production company's studios but the viewers had been mistaken.

Every stretch of water in Holderness was searched by the Police underwater team and on one occasion the body of a woman found on the North Yorkshire Moors was mistakenly linked with Gloria.

Anonymous letters and phone calls continued to arrive on Superintendent Carmichael's desk suggesting leads, one even saying Gloria had been sighted in Venezuela. A garden in Coltman Street was thoroughly searched but again with negative results.

Mike Blackburn still could not believe Gloria could have been seeing another man without him knowing! But neither he nor Gloria's parents could understand how she would leave and not let someone, somewhere, know where she was or at least that she was alive and well. However these are not views which were shared by Mrs. Jacqueline Clyne who was one of Gloria's closest friends and who worked with her.

"Gloria was a lovely person, Blonde, attractive enough to have been a model and great company. A real head-turner in a crowd.

Men loved her!" said Mrs. Clyne of Eastrington near Goole. The two of them often hit the local high life together, clubs, dances, Indian Restaurants — they went everywhere.

Jacqueline became very serious when she said, "Gloria was also capable of being very selfish. Having made arrangements to see you she would drop you at the last moment if something better came up. She always gave me the impression that if someone richer than her current boyfriend came along she might have gone off with him."

"A week or two before her disappearance she told me she was in a position to do something which would bring her a lot of money, about £30,000!! She wanted me to be bursting with curiosity and drag it out of her, but I was equally determined not to press her. In the end she didn't give me any further details but after she disappeared I was sorry I didn't show more interest."

"I still have nightmares about her", Mrs. Clyne concluded, "I often wake up in the night thinking about her. All I can say is that my life is so much duller since Gloria Bielby vanished!"

Eventually after a long and careful investigation Superintendent Carmichael was reluctantly forced to run the case down but the file still remains open. Gloria was a twin, attached to her parents and had a young son. It was quite out of character for her to have left home and failed to contact anyone again. The investigators still have to keep an open mind on the case. Is she abroad? Has she assumed a different name? Has she joined some religious sect? Has she re-married? Was she being blackmailed? Who was making the disturbing phone calls? The possibilities are endless but, more and more the great suspicion must be that she has been murdered! How and who knew about it?

There were many men in Gloria's life. Bernard her husband, Mike Blackburn and a host of others. Bernard himself finally divorced Gloria in January 1982 on the grounds of desertion.

Any man if provoked enough could have murdered her. Also many women would have become jealous of her. If one had discovered she was having an affair with their man, who knows what she might have done!

It is not beyond the bounds of possibility that a jealous man or woman hired a professional killer to dispose of Mrs. Bielby! Would it not be an amazing and sensational story if it transpired the man who picked her up on that fateful morning had been a hired assassin who had managed to worm his way into her affections to carry out his assignment! If Mrs. Clyne is right she was the sort of lady who could be tempted even though she had promised to marry Mike Blackburn!!

Maybe a much simpler motive was involved. A good con-man learning she was going to pick up a sum of £3,000 in 1979 could have been ruthless enough to lure her with the promise of even more, ten times the amount, and then kill for her £3,000!! What a tragedy if once again greed on the part of the victim was the cause of a very premature end to a beautiful woman!

If Gloria Bielby was murdered the murderer would have the problem of disposal of the body which of course has never been found. There are still ways and means of destroying all traces of a human body if one has the knowledge and access to the necessary equipment.

The case is one of the most baffling and intriguing left uncleared in this part of the country. It might never be resolved but human consciences are strange and it might still be difficult for those people who know, and there must be more than one, to keep such a dreadful secret!! As Bob Carmichael said when I spoke to him, "Who knows, this book may re-kindle some interest in poor Gloria. It would be so nice if the matter could finally be put to rest.

CHRISTINE MARKHAM — AGED 9 YEARS

On twentieth of May last year, 1995, Christine would have celebrated her 31st birthday. Sadly she vanished from the face of the earth twenty-two years before that could happen.

It was the day after her ninth birthday that her mother Mrs. Marjorie Markham waved to Christine and her brother and sister as they left their Robinson Road home in Scunthorpe, to go to school. Susan, Wayne and Christine, the youngest of the three, walked together until Christine left the others to go to her own school in Henderson Road.

The plump young girl was a happy child but was known not to be too fond of school and often played truant. She was also known as a bit of a tomboy. She didn't attend school on the fateful day after she left her brother and sister, neither did she ever return home again.

Her mother was used to her being late home. The child always claimed she had been playing with friends but when 7.30 pm passed and it became 8 o'clock she began to worry and sent three of her eldest children Graham, Susan and Carole to look for her. When they returned without her the increasingly worried mother began contacting relatives and friends in case she was with them. Finally in desperation she informed the police.

Police immediately began a full scale search and were joined by neighbours and friends. The searching went on throughout the night and continued despite a heavy thunderstorm.

As first light came with no success, police asked for military assistance and soldiers together with helicopters were brought in to assist with the searching. Fearing the worst, Lincolnshire's experienced Detective Chief Superintendent Miller Patrick took charge of the case and it was treated at a potential murder.

It seemed that the child had no intention of going to school when she left home. It was discovered that on two previous Mondays she had spent the day with her aunt Joan Shadlock who lived in Ashby. On the morning she disappeared she stopped a woman and asked which bus she should catch for Ashby. Coincidentally, her aunt was travelling the other way on a bus and thought she saw Christine pass in another bus. Realising where she might be going Mrs. Shadlock returned home but Christine was not there.

Altogether police recorded some 33 sightings of Christine Markham on the day she vanished. She was given twopence by a

HAVE YOU SEEN THIS GIRL?

IF SO, PLEASE CONTACT THE POLICE

MISSING GIRL

Missing from 21, Robinson Road, Scunthorpe, since 8.45 a.m. on 21.5.73.

Christine Deborah MARKHAM, 9 years, born 20.5.64.

Description: 3' 10", well built, fresh complexion, brown eyes, has a cast in eye. Ginger hair.

Dressed in plain, red, long sleeved dress, navy blue 'wet look' type coat, red socks and brown shoes.

This girl is a pupil of Henderson Avenue Junior School, but did not attend school on 21st May, 1973.

She was last seen at 7.30 p.m. on 21st May, 1973, in Henderson Avenue, near Hornsby Crescent, heading towards Ferry Road.

IF SEEN, please contact Scunthorpe Police Station, Telephone 3434 or any Police Officer.

Christine Markham.

71

Frogmen searching for Christine Markham.

woman in Long Road at about 10 am and soon afterwards persuaded another person to give her five pence to get the bus to Ashby. At one o'clock she was spotted near to a house where she used to live in Theodore Road and was seen numerous times during the afternoon.

It rained heavily during the evening but at 7.30 pm she was seen near Sheffield Park and the last recorded sighting was at 11 pm at the junction of Davy Avenue and Long Road.

The police hunt was a massive one and response from the public was spontaneous and generous. Everyone was naturally horrified that any harm may have befallen a young girl.

Information poured in of sightings of girls answering Christine's description. One was reported getting a lift on a tanker in company with a blonde girl and all tanker firms were contacted.

In June two anonymous persons offered £200 reward for information which would assist in the search and over 200 policemen were engaged searching the notorious Atkinson's Warren at Scunthorpe.

A report that she may have hitched a lift to the Norfolk coast immediately brought fears of a connection with the case of April Fabb, who had been missing from her home there since 1969 in suspicious circumstances.

Nearly six months went by and the intensive police activity had to be reviewed. No progress whatsoever was being made with either finding the child or establishing what had happened to her. It was decided to scale down the operation and Mr. Miller Patrick was firmly of the opinion that Christine Markham was dead!!

Two years later a diary was discovered tucked away at the side of a bar in the Oswald Hotel in Scunthorpe. It was a 1973 diary and inside was a letter alleged to have been written by Christine to a Steven, asking him to take her out! It was eventually put down by police as a hoax, a sick joke!

The file was never closed and still remains live in the records of Humberside Police. In 1975 the file was inherited by Detective Inspector Gerry Kendall when he moved to the town. He became fascinated with the case and determined to discover the truth if he could. He visited a number of prisons to interview sex offenders whose names had come up but was unable to make any progress. He knew that Chief Superintendent Patrick had given up the case in complete bafflement and after a careful study of all the facts he came to the following conclusions.

73

Christine did not leave Scunthorpe, neither was she abducted away from the town. She had not met with an accident otherwise her body would have been discovered. He felt that one of two explanations may account for Christine apparently vanishing from the face of the earth in May 1973 and both relate to major building work which was being done in the town at the time.

Large excavations existed on building sites and the child may have fallen and become trapped in one, or, because she frequented the sites, she may have been attacked and murdered by someone connected with the sites and buried in a way which would have made her discovery impossible. Many of the workers were not local men, were casual labour and came and went at will. The killer of Christine Markham if one exists could be anywhere!

This is one of the cases where it is unlikely that the end will ever be written with certainty and the Markham family will sadly continue to wonder what happened to their daughter and sister Christine.

EVELYN ROUNDING

It was only eight years after the Great War ended and the City of Kingston-upon-Hull was waiting expectantly for a visit from the popular Prince of Wales. Prince Edward was coming for a two-day stay on Tuesday and Wednesday.

Just off Beverley High Road was Fountain Road and the Rounding family lived at number 39. Mother kept house and helped the local midwife while Father was a joiner and rather clever amateur architect. Muriel Evelyn, the eldest daughter worked at Smith & Nephew. She was a bright girl and due to be promoted from factory to office the following Monday. Marjorie, the youngest

The River Hull where Evelyn Rounding may have died.

daughter was ten years old and still at school.

Friday 8th October 1926 was a normal day in the Rounding household and work had finished and tea had been consumed, after some desultory talk about the next week's royal visit, the pretty young Evelyn left the house to go out with friends. Both father and mother were strict with their girls who were expected to keep good company and proper hours.

The evening passed and Evelyn returned as normal and sat in a chair for a while before saying she was going to bed. When she got up, Marjorie moved to take the seat she had just vacated but soon realised it was wet. Not wishing to say anything she too rose to go to bed and her mother noticed the dampness on the chair. Accusing the youngest daughter of wetting herself she refused to listen to her denials and Marjorie received a good tanning. She was then made to put all her clothes and the chair and cushion covers into the dolly tub.

A very upset Marjorie lit her candle and went upstairs to the bedroom she shared with her elder sister. As she entered the room the flickering light showed that all of Evelyn's clothes appeared to be strewn around the room and as she passed by them it was obvious they were all wet.

The Saturday morning dawned and Marjorie woke and looked at her sister. She seemed very hot and looked pale and drawn. She was still asleep. Quietly getting out of bed Marjorie went downstairs and told her mother she thought Evelyn might be poorly. She also mentioned the wet clothes! Mrs. Rounding went up to the room and Evelyn woke. "What's up? Now tell me what's up?" demanded her mother. "What have you done? have you been misbehaving?" Evelyn's reply astonished her young sister. "I've taken some iodine!" she said.

Arrangements were immediately made to contact the doctor and within a very short time Dr. Jennings arrived on his pedal cycle. After examining the girl he turned to the mother and said, "You've no need to worry Mrs. Rounding, she's as pure as the day she was born!" "Told you I hadn't done nothing!" snapped Evelyn.

The doctor went downstairs and turned to the mother. "Now don't get on to her, she's suicidal. Just leave it at that."

As soon as the doctor left the house however, Mrs. Rounding ran upstairs and confronted her daughter. "Now, I want to know exactly what's been happening. I want to know what's been going on Evelyn!"

76

Evelyn said she had been for a walk along the river bank with a boy and he had tried to interfere with her and in the struggle she had rolled into the water's edge. She'd been a bit wet but nowhere near to being soaked.

Marjorie who had been listening open-mouthed to these dramatic happenings knew that the banks of the River Hull close to Beverley Road were a popular place for courting couples.

"Did you see her with any iodine?" Mrs. Rounding asked Marjorie. When the youngster replied in the negative her mother shook her head in perplexity. How had she got the iodine into the house without being seen?

Both mother and father were worried by Evelyn's behaviour, not only because of her apparent mental state but also because such things caused scandals in the neighbourhood and allowed the neighbours to talk. This was an even worse situation than their daughter's condition!!

Next day, Saturday, Mrs. Rounding kept a close eye on her eldest daughter but by the time Sunday arrived, Evelyn appeared to have recovered and was apparently none the worse for her experience. She was a very pretty girl with big blue eyes who used to dress smartly and Marjorie remembers how she used to wriggle her bottom as she walked. She was well developed and looked older than her age. All the boys were attracted to her.

As soon as tea was over on the Sunday, Marjorie was packed off to a neighbour's house to baby sit. Although only ten-years old herself she was considered mature enough to mind younger children.

Lily Londesborough who lived in Cave street came round to see if Evelyn was going out for a walk. Mrs. Rounding immediately refused permission but Evelyn was so obviously disappointed and thinking it might do her good she eventually relented and Evelyn left dressed in her Sunday best. Although it was October it was still warm enough for thin dresses and Summer hats.

Mr. and Mrs. Rounding later left for their weekly visit to the nearby Polar Bear public house. They would return as usual at 10 pm.

When they returned they were surprised to find that Evelyn was not in, although she had been given instructions to return by 9.30 pm. Stranger still was the fact that her bag was in the house indicating that she had been home and left again!

As time went on the family became more and more worried and the Police were informed. One strange factor emerged which was never satisfactorily cleared up. After Evelyn returned home that night, Mrs. Londesborough, Lily's mother, had visited 39 Fountain Road, on her own, and enquired if Evelyn was alright. The girl said she was and Mrs. Londesborough left. She refused to divulge why she paid this visit!! Police felt that Mrs. Londesborough had frightened the girl in some way and caused her to go and commit suicide!!

Lily's very comprehensive diary was found in her handbag but it revealed nothing about the previous Friday evening or about her state of mind. It was virtually full of details about various boys she knew or would have liked to know.

The Rounding's refused to tell anyone, including the police, about the incident on Friday night and the taking of the iodine, lest it involved them in scandal!

Nothing more was ever heard of Evelyn Rounding. The police dragged the river Hull without success and mother arranged for an S.O.S. to be broadcast on the BBC Home Service. The family listened in silence as the mournful tones of the announcer came crackling over their cat's whisker wireless.

A spiritualist consulted by Mrs. Rounding said the missing girl was in London. The distraught woman was willing to try anything and, taking the money saved for the Insurance man, she took the train to London and visited Scotland Yard. The kindly policeman on the enquiry desk there took details and promised they would keep a look out.

Within a week after the girl went missing Mr. Rounding's abundant black hair had turned white!

Possibly coincidentally, a few days after Evelyn's disappearance a seven-year old girl vanished from Hessle Road. She had been last seen standing on the Pier wearing her mother's wellington boots.

This could be nothing more than the suicide of a girl whose mental state had become disturbed. There are however a number of worrying factors which leave many questions unanswered, chief among them being — why did Mrs. Londesborough go to see Evelyn on the evening in question, and why would neither she nor her daughter Lily give a reason for the visit??

Maybe one or both of them are still alive and could still shed some light on the mystery!!

LOCAL MYSTERIES IN MODERN TIMES

Somebody killed these people! The killers are almost certainly alive today! Who are they??

The man who lived for rugby

Killing: Plea to caller

Murder probe man released

Gruesome river find

ATTIC RIDDLE UNSOLVED

'They had iron bars'

Coalman: Deserted house searched

COAL MERCHANT VANISHES ON HULL ROUND

EVELYN EDWARDS

In May 1966 the body of fifteen-year old Margaret Mowson had been found in a narrow lane known locally as 'Pig Alley' between Humber Street and Blanket Row in the City. She had been murdered by being struck violent blows on the head. A quiet girl, there was no suggestion she had been keeping bad company or of anything untoward in her background or character.

Chief Constable Walton was informed of this serious crime and cut short his holiday and returned to Hull. Always careful to avoid criticism and with major police amalgamation schemes in the air he decided to take no chances and to call in assistance from Scotland Yard, the first time this had been done in the City for 30 years.

Despite a massive police effort led by the Yard's Superintendent Leslie Rouse, the murder was not solved and a couple of days or so before the Inquest, Margaret's step-father received a chilling letter in which the writer claimed to be the killer and threatened to kill again. Despite this it was felt there was no useful point in keeping Superintendent Rouse in Hull and he returned to London.

Another Hull girl at the time was Evelyn Edwards. She was 18, pretty and with a happy personality, this latter trait the more surprising in view of her profession. But few of her prostitute friends, or her clients, knew that she was also epileptic and suffered blackouts.

Living at 85 Sykes Street in Hull, Evelyn was a twin and had been a perfectly normal child until an accident at Bean Street school had required a brain operation. Although she recovered well she was left with the legacy of epilepsy.

Soon after leaving school she took to the streets and became a familiar twilight figure in the Osborne Street red light area of the City.

At 5 am on Tuesday 21st March 1967, ten months after the body of Margaret Mowson had been found, and at a time of day when most night duty policemen would have been idling until the end of their shift, Sergeant Leslie Wilson, a naturally conscientious and energetic officer, was routinely checking a derelict three-storey

Derelict building on the corner of Osborne Street and Upper Union Road.

Evelyn Edwards.

building on the corner of Osborne Street and Upper Union Road known as 105 Osborne Street. Climbing some rickety stairs to the attic, he saw a heap of crumpled newspapers and on further examination discovered the body of a young woman.

His call for assistance resulted in the attendance of a doctor who certified life extinct and the head of the city C.I.D. Detective Superintendent Jim Cocksworth. This vastly experienced detective immediately ordered a major enquiry be set up and after the body had been examined by the Pathologist, Dr. Gee from Leeds, the whole scene was examined by forensic scientists and fingerprint officers, and the body was moved to the City Mortuary. Evelyn's mother attended and identified her daughter's body.

This was now extremely worrying for the chief constable. Not only was this the second young girl to have been violently done to death in Hull in a few months but threatening letters alleged to have been written by Margaret's murderer had been received by a number of young women since. He lost no time in once again asking for assistance from Scotland Yard. He rang the Assistant Commissioner (Crime) and a team was promised immediately.

C1 department of New Scotland Yard at the time housed about twenty experienced detective superintendents and their sergeants who had nominal jobs such as head of firearms, aliens etc., but whose main responsibility was to undertake investigations into serious crime, particularly homicide, when requested.

This time it was Superintendent Jack Weisner and Sergeant Robert Smith who collected their £100 initial expenses and set off for Hull. They arrived midday on Wednesday, the day after the body had been discovered.

All leave for Hull detectives had been stopped and the Metropolitan murder system was brought into operation. This system was basically a meticulous recording of every item of information on a card index with everything cross referenced.

Normal house to house enquiries had little relevance in the highly commercial area where the body had been found and initial enquiries were concentrated on Evelyn's background, her lifestyle, friends and associates and on activities in the murky world of Hull's prostitutes.

A post mortem examination on Evelyn's body was carried out by Dr. David Gee, Senior lecturer in Forensic Medicine at Leeds University. It revealed that death had probably occurred some days before the body had been found and that it was due to asphyxiation due to compression of the neck. Examination for sexual activity was irrelevant in view of the girl's way of life but there was no sign of violence.

It was discovered that Eveyln had left home on the Saturday before her body was found and she had eaten a meal in a local cafe at 7 pm the same day. The contents of her stomach corresponded with that meal thus indicating she died between the Saturday evening and the following day.

Massive efforts were made to trace and interview Evelyn's clients and her fellow prostitutes were closely questioned. As usual in cases where one of their number has been attacked and always conscious of the need to protect themselves in what was an extremely dicey way of life, the girls were unusually co-operative. It emerged quite quickly that Evelyn normally operated under the name Susan White!

An unusual and bizarre twist to the investigation came with information about a red car which Evelyn or Susan was alleged to have been seen in by some of 'the girls'! Soon traced, the car belonged to a senior NCO in the army at Leconfield Camp near Beverley.

Found on the girl's body had been a scrap of paper, apparently torn from a diary, with a telephone number scribbled on it. The number was that of one of Chief Constable Walton's neighbours!! When the army NCO was questioned he admitted the paper was from *his* diary.

He admitted picking a girl up he knew as Susan on the Saturday night and driving her to the Anlaby Road where they had sex. Returning her to Osborne Street she had asked him for a sheet of paper and he had given her a piece from his diary. He saw her write something on it.

Despite very close questioning and a detailed forensic investigation there was nothing to connect this man with the murder. After an initial excitement about the telephone number this too proved to be irrevelant.

A major break through occurred when in October, a young 17-year old shop assistant Sandra Carr was attacked in the bedroom of her lodgings in Louis Street in the city. The assailant, a 33-year old labourer Samuel Stephenson gave himself up the same day. When taken to the police station he surprised officers by not only admitting attacking two young girls in East Park but also being responsible for killing Margaret Mowson!

A search of his room revealed a bizarre collection of police and crime books together with threatening letters written and ready to post!

The Evelyn Edwards' team were cock-a-hoop. Doubtless this was their man also. But to their chagrin, despite a willingness to admit his crimes Stephenson denied outright anything to do with this case. There was nothing else to connect him!!

The rather dispirited officers continued the search for another man. They checked all the residents of the William Booth hostel and the company of a Royal Navy ship in dock at the time.

A further dampener was put on the enquiry when, at the Coroner's suggestion, Dr. Gee agreed there was a remote possibility the compression of Evelyn's neck could have been caused during an epileptic fit, by herself. But he added, this would be highly unusual.

The Coroner pointed out to the Jury that while the matter looked like murder, there was now a doubt and the possibility existed of a self-inflicted injury. The Jury, at his invitation, returned an open verdict.

Once this had been done Police felt happy to let the matter rest and write it off as natural causes. The investigation was wound down.

In hindsight, the balance of probability must be that Evelyn Edwards was killed. She would have been unlikely to have gone to the building on her own to have a fit!!!

ROBERT HAROLD STEVENSON

A sad and derelict house stands forlornly overlooking the restless Humber Estuary with the bustling Kingston-upon-Hull on the north bank now joined forever by the majestic Humber Bridge to the southern shore. Countless tides have moved up and down the restless estuary since the April week-end in 1969 when the occupant of the house, Harold Stevenson was found in a semi-conscious condition.

It had been a quiet April Wednesday in Barton-on-Humber. The ancient little township nestled just over the southern banks of the estuary and was the most northern point of Lincolnshire. Barton was as sleepy a little township as one could find in England, even the ferry across the Humber passed it by. There was talk of a bridge being built across the estuary but Sergeant Trevor Blackmore didn't think it would happen in his service!!

It was 1969 and he was one of two sergeants stationed at Barton. He was talking to the two constables on duty in the town's ancient police station and giving his opinion that they were unlikely ever to be visited by the I.R.A. One of the constables voiced the view that the Investiture of the Prince of Wales in Caernarvon in a month's time might well suffer from the attentions of the Welsh Nationalists. The casual gossip died and the sergeant was beginning to think of his tea when the telephone rang.

Constable Olsson answered and almost immediately signalled to the sergeant to listen. Farmer John Rigg from Barrow had found his landlord, Harold Stevenson, badly injured at his home. He appeared to have been attacked!

The sergeant knew Harold Stevenson. He was one of those nature's eccentrics, often found in isolated communities and whose manner of living was the subject of much talk in the area. About 70 years old, he lived as a semi-recluse at his home Holly Dene, Barrow Road, Barton.

The dwelling was in fact two cottages situated in an isolated position on the minor Barton to Barrow road. Surrounded by trees and outbuildings, the land sloped gently down to the bank of the river

Holly Dene, Barrow Road, Barton.

estuary and across the water Hull stood clearly as did the fire and smoke from the tall chimneys of oil terminal Immingham to the east. For some years a mother and daughter had lived in the second cottage and Harold was thought to be 'sweet' on the daughter. The two women had both died some years previously and since their deaths Harold had used the second cottage to store property he collected and bought. This was his abiding interest — collecting anything from good antiques to veritable junk.

His favourite method of acquisition was to attend auctions, wait until the end and offer a paltry sum to the auctioneers to buy anything left over!

As they approached the house the sergeant knew that every spare inch of the two cottages and the outhouses would be cluttered with the old man's possessions. The last time he had called, there had been about two dozen lawnmowers and even a bus stop sign.

On this day, Farmer John Rigg who rented land from Stevenson had gone to routinely pay his rent. Finding the back door open he had called out and thought he heard a groan from the front of the house. Concerned, he walked down the long passage and was faced by two doors set at an angle to each other. He could see the handles of each had been tied together on his side of the doors with what appeared to be an old scarf.

A peculiar and unnerving noise was coming from behind the door leading into the living room. The farmer nervously untied the door and then found it jammed from inside by clothes and old papers. Finally forcing his way in he saw Stevenson half sitting, half lying against the piano with what appeared to be a massive blood-caked wound on his head. Blood also covered his clothes. Without more ado the farmer rushed out to find a phone.

On arrival policemen were amazed to find that despite the frightful sight presented by the elderly man, he was still alive and conscious.

Sergeant Blackmore's report drawn up at the time records in true constabulary fashion what then took place. Almost unbelievably his first words were: "Now sir, are you alright?"

"Oh hello", mumbled Stevenson, stirring, "It's a long time since you came to see me!"

"How did you get down there, did you fall?" asked the Sergeant. A pause and the old man said, "I should think I must have done!"

Trying to gently move the injured man, the sergeant found he was unable to pull him away from the piano. He couldn't see what was making him stick to the instrument until he peered round the back of the body and to his amazement found that the man's braces had been nailed to the piano with six inch nails!!

"You've had a nasty bang on the head!", said the policeman examining the blood encrusted wound and trying to keep the old man calm.

Stevenson suddenly started rambling about demolishing property he owned in Hull and soon became incoherent. Mr. Rigg who had followed the police in and been standing in the hall shouted, "Never mind about that Harold, these chaps want to know what happened!"

Det. Ch. Supt. Joe Cammamile, head of Lincolnshire CID.

88

I don't know whether they were Chinamen or Irishmen!" came the sudden and unexpected reply. "There were two of them and they came with iron bars!"

In reply to further questions he thought the attack had been the previous Thursday when he came home from Hull but, when asked about the present day he had no idea what it was.

He was taken by ambulance to Scunthorpe Hospital and Sergeant Blackwell summoned assistance in what seemed likely to be a very serious crime indeed. Already it was attempted murder and it looked very doubtful if the old man could survive his injuries!

Detective Chief Superintendent Joe Cammamile, the then head of Lincolnshire C.I.D. and an experienced detective, arrived to take charge and over twenty detectives quickly mustered in the Court room at Barton Police Station for briefing.

Fingerprint examination revealed no useful prints but marks were discovered which very uniquely could be positively identified as being made by rubber gloves supplied only by Timothy Whites and Taylors, a national chain of chemists.

One strange aspect of the case was that the attackers had apparently collected a box full of groceries from the house and put them outside the door ready to take with them. Theft of food often suggests the involvement of either vagrants or persons on the run., Why they were left is difficult to understand. Were they disturbed?

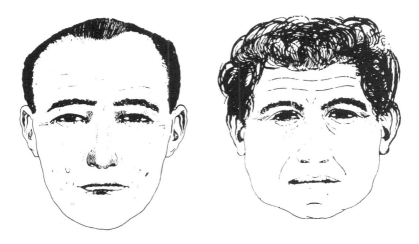

An artist's impression of two suspects.

Did they forget? Did only one man put them for himself and then think better of it? It remains a puzzling aspect to this day.

While the enquiry got under way and the team of investigators grew, the condition of Harold deteriorated and a week after being found he died of pneumonia caused by his injuries. He had spoken no more and his only evidence was that given to Sergeant Blackmore! This was now a very nasty murder case!!

One essential was to try and fix the time of the attack and the enquiry team became almost certain it was some time during the Saturday four days prior to finding the body.

The old man had been something of a Scrooge. He only had one pint of homogenised milk delivered each week; there was only one electric light bulb in the house; and he only had a paper delivered on Sundays. Even then the paper boy was given strict instructions not to leave the paper without having been given the money for it!

On the Sunday prior to the body being found and, possibly a few hours after the attack, the paper boy had tried to deliver the paper. Finding the door ajar and getting no response to his knocking he cautiously pushed the door open and had a view of the hallway with two closed doors at the far end. The boy's nervous dislike of the house was made worse when he thought he heard groaning from somewhere inside.

Deciding discretion was better than valour he closed the door and hurriedly made off. Too embarrassed, he told no-one of the experience until after Stevenson had been found. No-one could blame a young lad in those circumstances but the end of this case could have been so different had he reported his story!!

Another important question for the team was motive! The house had been ransacked and many trunks and boxes emptied in the room where the old man had been discovered. The place was in such a mess and with such an overwhelming amount of property it was impossible to be certain what, if anything had gone. Even had Stevenson himself been able to help, it could still have been a problem. The only thing that appeared to be missing was £8 in cash.

Motives for murder can usually be put into four well-known groups, greed, jealousy, revenge or fear. It is unlikely the latter two would have applied in this case. Harold was not the sort to instil fear or a need for revenge in anyone. Jealousy might possibly have been involved but if so it would almost certainly have involved the first motive — greed. A man living in Mr. Stevenson's circumstances always creates rumours, usually inferring that he is rich and that his riches are secreted at his home. Stories abounded locally that he had hoards of sovereigns and Dresden china in the house.

It seemed very likely the victim was correct in his recollection that two men were involved and that the attack occurred soon after he returned from a trip to his property in Hull.

Despite the thieves' attempt to steal household groceries the chances of a casual unpremeditated attack in such an isolated spot was unlikely and if he was followed on foot or in a car by thugs from Hull it would have been difficult for them as spasmodic ferry journeys would have been involved.

Despite a sustained and determined enquiry no progress was made with the investigation and it was gradually run down. No witnesses were found and no real suspects were ever identified.

Eighteen months after the murder the Corn Exchange at Brigg was full to overflowing with an unusually large crowd for the regular furniture auction. The fact that the possessions of the late Robert Harold Stevenson were going on sale had caused quite a stir.

Looking at the house and its contents at the time of the murder anyone could have been excused for thinking it was a load of junk.

Buyers at the sale of Mr. Stevenson's property.

91

When it came to be sold however it included some fairly valuable antiques.

In the event a large proportion of the crowd was merely there out of morbid curiosity and most of the property went to dealers.

In 1969 most provincial chief constables in a force the size of Lincolnshire would have called in New Scotland Yard to bring their expertise to bear on such an apparently intractable case. However Chief Constable George Terry decided against it and we shall never know whether that made any difference to the outcome.

The detectives leading the hunt were very depressed at their failure to solve the crime and dark mutterings continued for years afterwards in the Lincolnshire force, mainly about real or imagined shortcomings in the Hull police at the time. Rumours of conspiratorial failures in co-operation abounded. Such suspicions, often rife in county police forces when dealing with their urban colleagues were in fact unlikely to be true.

So who killed the old man so brutally? Did the murderers actually get something worthwhile which no-one has ever discovered? The determined and ruthless attack suggests that professional criminals took part. But local legend still has it that someone with local knowledge must have been involved. Where are the murderers now? Did they come from Hull, Grimsby, Scunthorpe, all of whom have their share of ruthless villains? Was it from further afield, Sheffield, Leeds? Or was it even closer to home in the quiet little town of Barton? Somebody knows and most likely still lives today — unlike their victim!!

WALTER TAYLOR

In 1996, eighteen years after her seventeen-year old son was found battered to death in a Scunthorpe playing field, his mother, Mrs. Joan Cuthbert's most fervent wish still is "I want it sorted before I die!"

Mrs. Cuthbert, previously Taylor, who remarried after the death of her first husband, recalls the day as if it was yesterday. It was 20th December 1978, her birthday. There were four Taylor children, Susan the eldest, Walter, Colin and Darren aged 9 years.

Walter, a non-driver who was learning to ride a moped was an apprentice insulation worker at Rilmac Engineering and enjoyed a quiet social life with friends in the Scunthorpe area. He wasn't into the drugs scene but Mrs. Cuthbert knew that together with most other young men of his acquaintance, he liked a drink or two.

The family lived in Victoria Road, Scunthorpe and as it was her birthday Walter went out in the evening and returned with a bottle of champagne. He didn't stop for tea but went straight out again shouting "Shan't be late, but make sure I'm up for work tomorrow!!" It was quite normal for him to go out for a night with his friends. She understood he was going to the Wortley Hotel to meet his mates. He was dressed in his black polo-necked jumper, royal blue jeans and black high-heeled cowboy boots.

Walter Taylor.

93

When he didn't return the next day it was assumed he had stayed with one of his mates. He didn't have a regular girlfriend but his mother was rather worried because she had a suspicion that he might have become involved with a married woman.

That morning she visited the Mill Road Club where she won some vouchers and then went to collect her Christmas turkey. While she was in the shop a lad asked, "Have you heard about the murder — a lad dressed all in black has been found dead!" After a moment's horrified silence, Mrs. Taylor whispered, "That's our Walter!" He had been dressed in what could have been described as all black on the evening he left home.

The body had been found at 5.45 am by three steel workers on their way to the factory. It was lying on its back and rather macabrely exactly in the middle of the centre circle of the football pitch in Jubilee Park. The face and head was covered with blood and a piece of tissue paper round the neck. Although a sports ground it was also used as an unofficial short cut home by many folk including the Taylor family.

Chief Supt. Crawley.

Chief Superintendent John Crawley, head of the county CID was soon on the scene together with Professor Alan Usher, the Home Office Pathologist from Sheffield. A mobile police sation with a 70-foot high radio mast was set up in nearby Lindley Street and engineers began running numerous telephone lines to the vehicle.

An examination revealed that the young man had died from severe head injuries and a piece of blood-stained Scots pine was found beside the body although it was never proved conclusively that this was the murder weapon. In fact it was the opinion of the Pathologist that the injuries could have been caused by heavy kicking. The tests also revealed that the

94

blood/alcohol level in the body was at least three times that permitted for driving.

Police soon discovered that the last time Walter was definitely seen was just after 10 pm on the 22nd when he left the Rabbit & Net

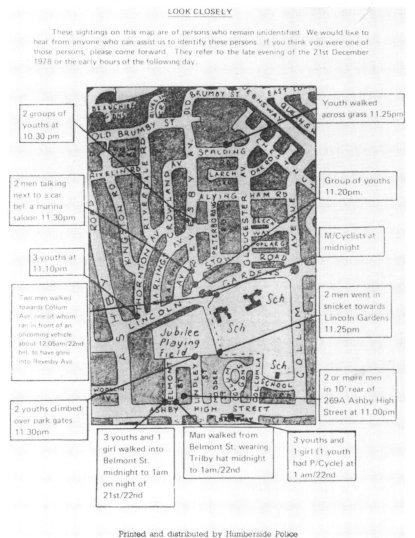

LOOK CLOSELY

These sightings on this map are of persons who remain unidentified. We would like to hear from anyone who can assist us to identify these persons. If you think you were one of those persons, please come forward. They refer to the late evening of the 21st December 1978 or the early hours of the following day.

2 groups of youths at 10.30 pm

Youth walked across grass 11.25pm

2 men talking next to a car bef. a marina saloon 11.30pm

Group of youths 11.20pm.

3 youths at 11.10pm

M/Cyclists at midnight

Two men walked towards Collum Ave. one of whom ran in front of an oncoming vehicle about 12.05am/22nd bel. to have gone into Revesby Ave.

2 men went in snicket towards Lincoln Gardens 11.25pm

2 youths climbed over park gates 11.30pm

2 or more men in 10' rear of 269A Ashby High Street at 11.00pm

3 youths and 1 girl walked into Belmont St. midnight to 1am on night of 21st/22nd

Man walked from Belmont St. wearing Trilby hat midnight to 1am/22nd

3 youths and 1 girl (1 youth had P/Cycle) at 1 am/22nd

Printed and distributed by Humberside Police

Different sightings mapped out by the police.

95

(Scunthorpe Community Centre). At about 11.55 pm the same evening, a young man who answered Walter's description was seen staggering along Old Brumsby Street towards Revesby Avenue. He leant over a garden wall and appeared to be trying to vomit. If this was in fact Walter, where had he been between 10 pm and nearly midnight??

At least ten sightings of people, either singly or in groups were recorded in the relevant area between 10.30 pm and 1 am on the night in question who may or may not have been involved in the murder. Amazingly, despite massive publicity asking for them to come foward, their identities still remain a mystery to this day.

The police operation was one of the biggest ever seen in the area. There had been no undetected murders in South Humberside since the formation of Humberside police in 1974 and John Crawley did not want this to be the first. House to house enquiries were made over a wide area. An initial reward of £1,000 was soon increased threefold by the local Chamber of Commerce and over 8,000 people were soon to be interviewed but with no result.

Constant publicity was maintained and the town's newsagents willingly co-operated by delivering over 30,000 leaflets asking for information and stressing the reward on offer.

Walter's mother maintained a determined campaign of her own, constantly appealing for help in discovering her son's murderer and while happy with the local police efforts, became so frustrated she asked if Scotland Yard could be called in to bring fresh minds to bear. The call was rejected by the Authorities who were convinced local police had all the expertise necessary to solve cases if at all possible.

As time went on different detectives took over the hunt. The best brains in the force were brought to bear — Godfrey Waddington, Ron Smith, David Watson, all tried. Time went on, still police doggedly persisted with the case. All were frustrated in their efforts and failed to solve the baffling mystery.

No motive was ever established for the crime. Walter Taylor was not an aggressive type of lad, not the sort to get involved in fights but could have become so intoxicated he just got into a drunken brawl. But such brawls very seldom end in deaths.

Many possibilities remain unresolved. Robbery can be ruled out as there was no apparent attempt to steal from the dead man. Was he in some ordinary scrap and left by the assailants who assumed he

96

The house in Victoria Road, Ashley,
where Walter Taylor lived.

was alright and would recover? Did he have a secret liaison with a married woman? Had he seen her on that fateful evening? Was this some form of revenge attack by her relatives or friends?

More than one person was probably involved and they are undoubtedly still alive today. Quite marked blood stains would have been present on clothing and by now more and more people will, for one reason or another, have become aware or suspicious of the identify of the assailant(s). The evidence in the case is still carefully preserved — the case can go ahead — the one small break the police are waiting for can, and probably will, still come to light. The perpetrators should still not sleep easily in their beds! Walter's death may still be avenged and his mother's mind put to rest, once and for all.

OLIVE WILKINSON

In 1983 the area around Montague Street in the holiday resort of Cleethorpes was very run down and a far cry from the glitzy promenade and hotel areas. It was home to many of the area's unfortunately, squatters, tramps, alcoholics, drug users and with a fair sprinkling of criminals all living in what was often semi derelict property alongside ordinary hardworking folk.

Twice divorced Olive lived with her daughter Michelle in relative comfort amidst all the squalor surrounding their home. She had five children from her failed marriages.

Friday 10th June 1983 was the day after Margaret Thatcher had been returned to power for what was to become her last term as Britain's Prime Minister. More importantly for Olive it was her day to collect her Giro and the day started quite normally for her. She called Michelle at 7.30 am and saw her off to work at 8.20. Michelle worked at the nearby Ramsden's supermarket.

As often happened, neighbour David Wilkinson who was not related, called round for a cup of coffee soon after Michelle left home and an hour and a half later, Olive left the house to go to her mother's house, after arranging to meet David later in a local pub.

At 11.50 am Michelle arrived home for her dinner and on entering

Montague Street.

98

the house was stunned to be confronted with the body of her mother, lying face down on the floor of the living room. She had died from massive head injuries.

Immediately a major police investigation was started under the local head of C.I.D. — Detective Chief Inspector Ted Greenheld. Over the following twelve months over 150 officers were to be involved at one time or another in trying to solve this savage murder. Two and a half thousand statements were taken and £1,000 reward offered for information, but despite all this effort the case remained unsolved!!

Every modern scientific communication technique was brought to bear on the case but nothing and nobody could throw any light on what had happened to Olive between leaving her house at 9.40 am and being found by her daughter just over two hours later. Apart from one sighting of her leaving home on the route she would have taken to the local post office, no-one except the murderer is known to have seen her afterwards!

Her Giro money was paid out by the post office although nobody there could actually remember serving her. Where did she go? What did she do? Who did she speak to? These are questions that remain unanswered today. She didn't visit her mother as intended and she didn't turn up at the pub to meet David Wilkinson.

The normal possible suspects, boyfriends, ex husbands etc. were quickly seen and all eliminated. The forensic examination of the scene revealed nothing except a solitary fingerprint which had not been made by people with legitimate access to the premises.

A process of fingerprinting all males between 16 and 60 in the area was undertaken and subsequently the area covered was widened more and more but without success.

Eventually after 2 years of maximum effort the police were forced to admit defeat and wound down their enquiries. The files remain intact to be re-opened immediately any significant clues come to hand.

Olive Wilkinson was 36-years old when she was murdered, registered as a blind person she had to wear thick pebble glasses to see. She had not been sexually assaulted by her attacker and apart from her Giro income had little wealth to steal. With sex and robbery put aside it is difficult to understand why anyone should want to kill a woman so violently. Was she making demands on someone? Did someone lose their temper about something? Was

Ch. Insp. Greenheld briefs his team.

some form of jealousy involved?

Someone killed Olive Wilkinson in mid-summer 1983. Who was it and where are they now? A killer remains at large somewhere **—they may be known to you.**

SUSAN DRURY

The Christmas spirit was well and truly abroad in Scunthorpe as Christmas 1985 approached. At 5.45 pm, on the 23rd December twice married, 40-years old Fred Drury, walked his 24-years old wife Susan to Sheffield Street in the town because she was going to stay with friends in Dale Street. After leaving her and visiting some friends himself, Mr. Drury returned home to Holland Avenue and just after 10 pm went to bed. His wife had not returned home when he retired.

At 9.30 am the following morning, Christmas Eve, the postman was delivering to the Drury's house when he noticed a heap in the front garden. His worst suspicions were soon confirmed — the body of a woman was lying behind a fency only eight freet from the road. It was Susan and she was dead!!

The alarm was raised and a massive police operation swung into operation under the local CID chief, Detective Superintendent Ted Greenheld. Fred Drury, hastily dressed, was taken to Scunthorpe Police station and it was obvious he was being treated as a suspect by the investigators when they kept him there for the next 30 hours.

Susan Drury.

Police found a strange situation existed when they made enquiries among Susan's relatives, all of whom lived in Scunthorpe. They were most reluctant to talk about Susan or themselves.

It was known she had been married previously but had cohabited with Fred Drury for about four years before they finally married in 1983. It was reputed to have been a very stormy marriage.

There was to be no leave for the police officers involved over

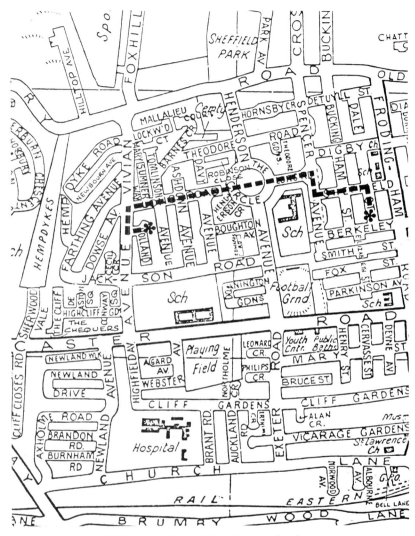

A map of the route taken by Mrs. Drury on her last journey.

the Christmas and New Year period and although the holiday period made enquiries more difficult the operation continued at maximum pace. On 5th January Fred Drury was dramatically re-arrested on suspicion of murdering his wife and kept in custody for a further 36 hours before being released again with no charge having been made.

On 14th January police re-enacted Susan's believed movements in the hours before she was killed. A 26-year old Special Constable retraced the journey, in an eerie darkness with heavy rain pouring down.

There were no developments and on 17th January Fred Drury made a dramatic public outburst alleging that police and public were pre-judging the situation and accusing him of being a murderer. He claimed he had been subject to assaults by people in the streets and that, together with a 24 hour police surveillance the situation was driving him crazy!

He thought his wife's body had been dumped in the garden from a car after 1 am on the Christmas Eve. He fixed the time from the fact his neighbours had been watching television in the front room until then and would have seen anything happening in his front garden before they went to bed.

Just two months later the most bizarre twist in the story occurred. Arraigned before the Crown Court at Lincoln was Fred Drury, charged with aggravated burglary and wounding with intent at the house in Dale Street to which his wife had been going when he left her a few hours before her murder. This serious crime had taken place on September 25th — three months almost to the day before Sandra's body was found!! Prosecuting Counsel Stuart Rafferty takes up the story and says:

"Drury married his young wife Susan in 1983 and one could imagine that the difference in age might lead to difficulties in due course. Theirs was a marriage with a fair share of difficulties. She would leave him to stay with friends and he was not happy about it. He thought she would face out her problems. The pattern seemed to be that there would be an argument, she would leave him and would then come back.

Mrs. Drury again left home in September and went to stay with Gordon and Marie Pook for longer than usual. Drury visited Dale Street several times to persuade his wife to return but she refused. She did however sleep with Drury one night when he visited Dale Street and was asked to stay for a meal.

After a blazing row at Dale Street on 25th September, Drury returned to the house at night and broke in. He crept into Mrs. Pook's room while his wife was asleep in another room only yards away. It was after 2 am and Drury had gone there for one reason and one reason only", said the barrister.

Mrs. Pook awakened when she felt Drury touch her as he knelt on her bed. After trying to strangle her and then smother her with a pillow he began attacking her with a knife, repeatedly trying to stab her in the chest. Mrs. Pook was screaming and trying to ward off the blows with her forearms. She managed to roll over and was immediately stabbed in the back. Eventually she managed to evade the blows and ran screaming into Susan's room while Drury escaped.

A short time after the attack Drury was alleged to have turned up at Scunthorpe Police station, pale and shaking and sweating heavily. His clothes were drenched in blood. he said that he'd been to Mrs. Pook's home to give her a good hiding but denied having used a knife!

The trial continued for three days and while Drury admitted 'thumping' Mrs. Pook he denied using a knife. His defence was based on allegations that Mrs. Pook was encouraging his wife to go there and to sleep with other men. He claimed this was driving him crazy. He was wild with jealousy, tormented and tortured by his wife's infidelity and fickleness.

Fred Drury, handcuffed, arriving for his wife's funeral.

Drury claimed that another man had threatened Susan with a knife after making sexual advances to her and claimed that Mrs. Pook encouraged Susan to have sex with that man and another one.

He was found not guilty of the serious offences he was charged with but guilty of unlawful wounding and simple burglary.

In mitigation his counsel revealed for the first time that Susan Drury had been found murdered a few months previously and suggested that Drury's future was very bleak, he had lost his wife. He lived for her and there was now very little left. He has nothing to live for! A Psychiatrist called for the defence said Drury was suffering from pathological jealousy when he attacked Mrs. Pook. He was jailed for two and a half years.

Of course when police had been called to the Drury's house that fateful Xmas Eve they were already aware of the impending court appearance and the sort of thing he was capable of.

Despite every effort by detectives the murder of Susan Drury has never been solved. When her body was at last released for burial on 8th June 1987 Fred Drury followed the coffin handcuffed to Prison Officers who had escorted him from Stafford Prison!!

FLORENCE MILLS

Wednesday, 19th April 1989 was a typically English early Spring day. It was rather cold and overcast with the sun occasionally peeping through heavy clouds. The banks of the Humber Estuary were empty of people except for a lone man walking his dog along the southern shore near South Ferriby at a spot known as Pebbly Beach. The steelworker was glad of any open air after a shift in the works at Scunthorpe! He glanced casually at the dog sniffing what looked like a lump of wood but as he came nearer he realised to his horror, it was a rotting human head. Hastily leaving the spot the man telephoned police.

They were quickly on the scene, as was Professor Alan Usher and an examination of the gruesome find was started. There was no obvious evidence of identification present and details were circulated to all forces whose area bordered the Humber or its tributaries, requesting that missing person files be searched.

But other forces need not have bothered, the answer was very

Humber foreshore at South Ferriby where Florence Mills' head was found.

near at hand! Florence May Mills, twice married and living at Melbury Walk, Scunthorpe had been reported missing since Good Friday, March 31st 1988 and dental records, hair samples, oral probes and a single stud earring proved conclusively it was her.

Normally police treat reports of adult missing persons with some caution. Many, particularly women, leave home unexpectedly to start new lives without coming to any harm. But strangely the report of Mrs. Mills disappearance had been treated very differently! Immediately a full scale enquiry was launched, over 1000 man hours were eventually spent making enquiries and conducting large scale searches of the area known to have been frequented by the lady.

Why was this case treated so differently? Investigators were very cagey about the whole affair but the finding of the severed head over a year later certainly confirmed their worst fears. The forensic report indicated that the head had been cleanly severed from the torso by either a knife, a cleaver or a saw. It was murder and the murderer presumably thought dismemberment would hinder identification!!! The remainder of the body has never been found. It too could have been put in the river and taken out to sea by the currents or perhaps disposed of in some other manner. The cause of death could not be determined from the head alone but Professor Usher felt that severe blows which had been inflicted to the rear of the skull could have been the cause. They had been made with a heavy blunt instrument.

Mrs. Mills' background turned out to be somewhat unusual, not to say eccentric. Her first marriage to a Mr. Tacey had seen her as a normal mother who brought up a family in a caring way and she was normally a creature of habit. She regularly picked up her pension or other allowances at Frodingham Road post office and the day prior to vanishing she spoke to her daughter and arranged to meet her the following day..

Police enquiries revealed some unusual facts however. Mrs. Mills was fond of a local area known as Atkinson's Warren and had been known on occasions to sleep out there at night. She had secretly married her second husband, James Mills on St. Valentine's day 1987, had split up with him after only five months, yet despite this, on the last day anyone was known to have seen her she was outside her second husband's home in Grosvenor Street and told a neighbour she was thinking of moving back in with him!!

There was about forty thousand pounds to her name in bank and building society accounts and this was untouched. She had a car and

James Mills.

Florence Mills.

two months after she disappeared it was privately sold!! She was living in a flat at Melbury Walk but on April 4th, four days after she went missing, the Council received a letter from her saying she was moving out. Police dismissed the strange timing of the arrival of this letter as probably caused by nothing more sinister than the Easter Bank Holiday posting arrangements.

Apart from enquiries in the area where she lived and among her family and friends, the main search for Mrs. Mills was concentrated on the Atkinson's Warren area. Over fifty officers together with specially trained dogs were brought in and spent hours examining the thickly wooded area.

Both Superintendent Geoff Smith and Chief Inspector David Watson spent hours on the case but although they suspected the worst, little progress could be made without a body. Gradually as leads ran out and time went on the enquiry had to be run down. Then, just a over a year after her disappearance, the gruesome find was made on the banks of the Humber.

Why would someone want to spirit away a harmless grandmother and murder her? One would think it unlikely to have been unpremeditated and yet — stranger things have happened since. An elderly grandmother was stabbed to death in a remote rural part of the north bank, near Burton Fleming in the early part of 1995.

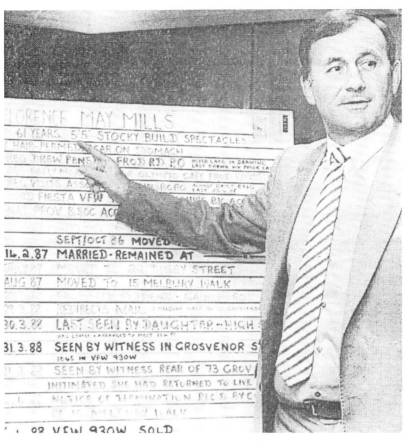

Det. Supt. Geoff Smith briefing his team.

Again no apparent motive! Who would do such things? Is it one and the same person?

Why would the body have been dismembered? Was the torso also cut up into pieces? Was it just an attempt to avoid identification or was there a more macabre and sinister reason behind it??

The eventual Coroner's Inquest could do no more than return an Open Verdict. Humberside Police at still hoping, indeed are optimistic, that an answer to Mrs. Mills' death will be found. One has to wonder what they knew at the outset of Mrs. Mills' disappearance which caused such a massive police operation to find her!!!

110

Police and dogs searching for a body.

KEITH EDWARD SLATER

Barrie Lilley was fast asleep at about 1 am on Sunday 27th August 1988 when the telephone rang. Muttering irritably the head of the area CID answered and was immediately all attention. A man had been killed by a stabbing in Bon Accord Road, Hessle, on the western outskirts of Hull. His wife was stirring as he dressed and to this day he ruefully recalls saying to her "Ah well, at least this shouldn't take too much clearing up!" It still remains unsolved over eight years later!!

Twenty-five year old Keith Slater was a driving instructor, living with his wife Carol in a quiet part of the village and he was also known as a keen and popular member of Hessle Rugby Union club.

On arrival at the scene Superintendent Lilley soon discovered that the attack had been just after midnight. The Slaters had been in bed when the bell on the front door rang. Sleepily Keith had made his way

Keith Edward Slater.

downstairs and opened the door. Carol heard the sounds of a disturbance and Keith shouting. Running down she found her husband lying on the garden path, obviously in great distress and at the same time saw the figure of a man running away down the road. She immediately dialled 999 and alerted police.

Neighbours were awakened by the noise and they too saw the figure of a man running away towards Buttfield Road. Keith Slater had died from a single stab wound without speaking a word.

The police murder routine swung smoothly into action, the scene was sealed and meticulously searched, the backgrounds

112

Bon Accord Road.

and movements of the dead man and his family were investigated and all his friends, associates and business and social contacts identified for interview.

A description of the suspect was compiled and circulated and the route he had apparently taken from the scene was identified and searched. A blood stained tissue was found which indicated the assailant had probably used a footbridge to the Hessle foreshore of the Humber Estuary. The assailant was described as white, in his mid 20s, between 5′6″/8″ with light coloured spikey hair like a brush and wearng a dark coat, dark trousers and a round necked light coloured "T" shirt.

Keith Slater had been a good looking active young man who, although owning his own motor car, was franchised to Haltemprice Driving School. His financial circumstances were examined and found to be normal. He was neither poor nor rich. Socially he did not go out a lot but mainly spent time with friends associated with Hessle Rugby Club.

Quite a few sightings of a man answering the suspect's description were soon uncovered. Ten days prior to the attack an unknown man of similar description was asking about Slater's whereabouts at the rugby club. On the day of the murder another man, possibly the same one, was enquiring the whereabouts of Bon Accord Road. These incidents suggested the person knew something about Slater, i.e. he was a member of the club and that he lived at Bon Accord.

113

Artist's impression of the assailant.

The lengthy examination of the scene revealed few clues. One unidentified fingerprint was found on an internal door and the amount of blood indicated the killer's clothing was bound to be bloodstained. but could well have been hurled into the waters of the Humber.

If a motive could have been discovered the investigation would have been a lot easier and the detectives had to look at all possibilities.

Had the murdered man been involved with another woman? He mixed socially at Hessle Golf Club where rumours of wife swopping were rife at the time. He also had many female driving students. The theory was supported by the discovery of a number of alleged sightings of him, in his car, in circumstances unlikely to be related to

The footpath believed to have been used as escape route by the murderer.

his work, but with a strange woman! These sightings were in the days prior to his death.

On the 15th August, twelve days before the murder, he had been seen at the junction of Barrow Lane and Swanland Road, Hessle. On the morning of 25th, only two days before he died he was spotted with a female in his car at the junction of First Lane and the Boothferry Road and at 5 pm on the day prior to the attack he was again seen but this time parked on Springfield Way. It was also reported that Slater found the tyres of his car had been slashed one day. While this might have just been mindless vandalism it could also indicate somebody had a nasty grudge against him!! The slashing had taken place in the car park of the West Bulls public house where, it was claimed, Slater had been seen on a number of occasions with an unknown woman. He was also reported as being seen in the National pub in the same area of Hull as the West Bulls.

Certainly Keith Slater's movements on the day before he died gave no reason to suspect anything out of the ordinary was going to happen. He got up with his wife and two children at 9 am and they all went fishing in the morning. They had a picnic by the Humber

Map of Hessle in the vicinity of the victim's home showing sightings of assailant and his escape route

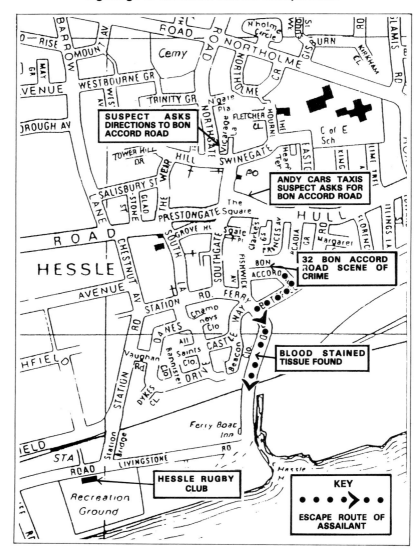

Bridge at lunchtime. He gave a number of driving lessons in the afternoon and evening, picked his wife up from work at Homebase in Hessle and after doing a bit of shopping they returned home and he retired at 11.30 pm.

By now Superintendent Lilley was beginning to realise the case was not going to crack easily and more detectives were brought in. At one time over a hundred were engaged on what was becoming a baffling case.

Police learned that Carol Slater had once worked at Willersley House and had become friendly with a man there. The man had subsequently gone to London. Thinking he might wish to harm Keith for some reason, police traced his whereabouts and arrested him for questioning. He could not be connected.

The Slaters were also friendly with another couple, the man being another Haltemprice instructor. It was alleged that Keith Slater had become very friendly indeed with the wife, as a result of which her husband left her feeling extremely upset by Slater's conduct. This seemed likely to be a fruitful line of enquiry and the man was arrested and questioned at length. He claimed to have been staying in a seedy hotel in the Paddington area of London on the night in question with a girlfriend. Staff at the hotel were seen and could remember the girlfriend but not the man!!! However if it had been this man who murdered Keith Slater, Carol Slater would have almost certainly recognised him.

There was a possibility the murder could have been a hired 'hit-man' job and two possible suspects were brought in for questioning but could verify their whereabouts on the night in question. They were working as bouncers at a local club!!

Altogether a total of seventeen men and four women came under suspicion at one time or another in the enquiry and were either arrested or interviewed as suspects in the case.

Nearly 10,000 police man hours and £100,000 was spent on the investigation.

It is felt strongly among the investigation team that they got quite close to the answer but not close enough to take proceedings against anyone. That little extra required for a murder charge could still come to hand. A vicious and callous murderer cannot be allowed to walk free for ever!!

CONCLUSIONS

This book has recounted just a few of the unsolved mysteries in a fairly small area of the country during the nineteenth and twentieth centuries. Many more people have been unlawfully killed in the same area over the same period but an overwhelming proportion of these cases has been solved and the offenders dealt with in an appropriate fashion by our Courts.

Unfortunately there will always be murders and sinister disappearances and some will remain unresolved. It may be that by writing this book someone's memory somewhere will be triggered which will lead to one or more of the cases described being cleared up. That would be a bonus indeed, especially in relation to the more recent ones.

Most murders are committed as a result of some connection between the victim and murderer — the overwhelming majority of the population will never come into contact with such a case let alone be a victim. There is more chance of being struck by lightning than being murdered. So, as they say on TV's Crimewatch — sleep well. don't have nightmares!